Jimmy Stewart

Biography

The Untold Story of the Life and Career of a Film Icon

CONTENT

Chapter 1: How the Stewarts Won the West

Chapter 2: Defeat the Kaiser

Chapter 3: Education and inventions

Chapter 4: The Lady's Gentleman

Chapter 5: Taking the Center Stage

Chapter 6: Hollywood

Chapter 7: What Are We Going to Do With Jimmy Stewart?

Chapter 8: Star Status

Chapter 9: A Commission and an Oscar

Chapter 10: Trying to Live a Wonderful Life

Chapter 11: The Unknown FBI Agent

Chapter 12: Friendships are renewed and destroyed

Chapter 13: The Last Beneficial Decade

Chapter 14: The Television Years

Chapter 15: Honoured until the end

Chapter 1: How the Stewarts Won the West

James Maitland, the round, bouncing infant boy Stewart was born to Alexander and Bessie Stewart on January 20, 1908, in Indiana, Pennsylvania. Alexander, popularly known as Alex, was born into a vast family of pioneers who established in Pennsylvania.

During the American Civil War, which lasted from 1861 to 1865, Justice of the Peace Archibald and his younger brother, James Maitland, enlisted in the Union Army. Seven of John Kerr Stewart's grandsons also fought in the Civil War. 'When my grandfather and other members of the family participated in the Civil War,' Jim explained, 'it created a strong heritage of military involvement in the Stewarts.' This was a practice that eventually drove James Stewart to forsake cinema and join the United States Army Air Force at the outbreak of World War II. Jim's heroes appear to have included Archibald and James Maitland.

James Maitland returned from the battle to marry Virginia Kelly, the daughter of a Mexican battle veteran. Her grandpa had been a state senator, and her great-grandfather had served in the American Revolutionary War. James and Virginia had two boys, Alexander and Ernest, the latter of whom was born with a deformed leg.

James Maitland should have been troubled at some point in his life. Virginia died of a sickness when she was young, and a second wife also died before her time. His religious beliefs were put to the test, but he always seemed to come out stronger. Such blows to his life, however, seemed to impair his geniality, and he appeared to have moments of bitterness and wrath.

His son Alex (James Stewart's father) received a good education, attending the best institutions his father could afford, such as Mercersburg Academy in southern Pennsylvania's Cumberland Valley and Princeton, a university with strong ties to the Presbyterian

Church. Then, in April 1898, just weeks before getting his Science degree, he enlisted in the Pennsylvanian Volunteers to serve in the Spanish-American War.

Alex's experiences during the war were long a source of speculation, even for his son Jim. 'What I do know is that he spent seven months of the conflict in San Juan, Puerto Rico's capital. People said he was in the battle for San Juan Hill in Cuba, and he never denied it. But he couldn't quite corroborate it either.'

According to Gloria, Alex's tendency for fantastic tales rubbed off on Jim. There were the stories Jim told journalists and on television for the sake of amusement, she explained, and then there was the truth. She went on to say that much of the truth was as amusing as the "tall stories." Gloria became a trustworthy source for the veracity of Jim's many stories. 'He's a brilliant storyteller, and he can launch into one of his yarns... and then he stumbles-that is, he suffers some misfortune-just at the appropriate point,' said actor Burgess Meredith, a long-time friend of Jim's. It's ideal timing, because the stumble and pause before the catastrophe are what make it a crowd-pleaser, so to speak. Jimmy fumbles in his narrative to make his own misery the punch line, satirising himself.' According to my observations, Jim's yams ranged from the factual to the overblown, with the occasional bit of hilarious fabrication thrown in for good measure.

Alex went on to demonstrate that he was anything from mentally disabled. The esteem and respect he (and Jim) had for James Maitland were unaffected by the elderly man's unpleasant demeanour. Alex's father had always expected him to work in the Big Warehouse, and he did not disappoint. For several years, he worked as his father's employee until 1905, when he was able to purchase a one-third stake in the store, a sensible economic decision that more than satisfied James Maitland.

'Dad was a colourful guy with a common touch that appealed to many of the clients,' Jim said of his parents. Mom was a well-educated, elegant, and polite lady. They didn't resemble each other at all. But they had love and respect for one other, and they loved each other.'

Alex and Bessie married on December 19, 1906, and the first of their three children, James Maitland Stewart, was born two years later, on January 20, 1908. The second child, a daughter called Mary Wilson (from Bessie's side of the family), was born on January 12, 1912, and Virginia Kelly (named after her father's mother) was born on October 29, 1914. They lived near the store on Philadelphia Street, but when the family grew, Alex relocated them to 104 North Seventh Street in the Vinegar Hill neighbourhood. 'My parents lived there for the rest of their lives, and it was always home to me, even though I didn't reside there until much later in life,' Jim recounted. It was always comfortable.'

'Jim's mother had a lifelong hearing impairment that Jim inherited by the time he was middle-aged,' Gloria told me in one of our numerous discussions between 1979 and 1994. Bessie spoke slowly and methodically in order to ensure that she was understood. And Jim assumed it was her way of adjusting for her hearing loss. She'd make an effort to talk slowly and deliberately. As Jim grew older, he found himself mimicking her speech patterns, which is how he began to talk with his distinctive drawl. People believe it's because he thinks slowly at times. However, he is not. He's razor-sharp. However, when he speaks, you can almost see him thinking ahead, which delays his delivery. And as he's gotten older and lost a lot of his hearing, it's become more pronounced, so the audience now has the James Stewart they know and love [in the late 1970s and 1980s]. Cynics believe it's all a ruse. The uninformed believe he is not very bright. They're completely wrong.'

Jim, like many of the Stewarts before him, grew up with a deep faith in God, which was instilled in him from birth: 'Religion was a vital part of our life. We used to go to church rather frequently. The Presbyterian Church is a Christian denomination. My mother sang in the choir and my father played the organ.

This component of Jimmy Stewart's family life is what made him a man who was adored as a human being by millions of people all over the world, not just as a movie star. 'There's no doubt that Jim's religious background helped to bring out his values, which he still has now,' Gloria said in 1979. It is what distinguishes him as a decent, honourable, and patriotic human being.'

It's also likely that Reverend Hinitt's preaching on racial tolerance kept Jim from becoming a racist. Pennsylvania has a history of racial intolerance and was long a favourite gathering place for the Ku Klux Klan, but the Reverend's words must have helped Jim keep his prejudice in check.

Alex Stewart was well-known in Indiana not only for being a colourful, good-natured man or for running the Big Warehouse, but also for becoming involved in everything he thought a good citizen of any town should get involved in. He was a Mason, a member of the Indiana Rotary Club, and a member of the Salvation Army's advisory council. What piqued Jim's interest was the fact that his father was a volunteer firefighter.

Chapter 2: Defeat the Kaiser

While many actors grow up with a burning desire to tread the boards or grace the silver screen, Jim did not: 'I never had any ambition to be an actor when I was a youngster. It never occurred to me.

Even watching movies had no influence on young Jim other than to keep him entertained. 'I don't think watching movies back then had much of an impact on anyone's objectives,' he remarked. They were just the fluttering images you saw on nickelodeons. People who wanted to be actors back then probably did so because they enjoyed the excitement of performing in front of an audience.

'There was an actress called Ruth Roland... she was one of the silent screen's great heroines in a long run of serials,' Jim said of the flickering movies. She was, I suppose, my first fantasy woman. My favourite actress was her. She wasn't the greatest actress of all time, but she was my favourite movie star.

While Jim was growing up and becoming more interested in the world, Europe was at war. It never occurred to Jim that the war would have any direct impact on him, other than instilling in him what would become his life's greatest passion--a aeroplane. 'During the Great War, I became quite interested in planes. I was approximately nine years old... and we used to get a magazine called Literary Digest, and most issues seemed to feature photographs of the war on the cover. And every time there was an image of an aeroplane, I carefully took the cover off and placed it on my bedroom wall until the wall was completely covered in aviation pictures. There was no better fantasy for a dreamer than the power to fly. And I began to fantasise about flying... about being free like a bird... about being able to look down on the world from a great height and possibly see it as God sees it.

The conflict also inspired him to make plays, but he said he still had no ambitions to be an actor: 'Doing plays was simply me having fun. I started putting on shows for other people... in our basement. I believe that many children do this without having any theatrical ambitions. For no other reason than it was enjoyable, I put on a production in our basement called Beat the Kaiser... and I wrote, produced, directed, and played all the male characters. My sisters played the female characters. And I made Mom and Dad sit and observe. I recall thinking Dad looked swollen and red in the face, and I assumed he was just unwell. Years later, I realised he constantly looked like that while he was trying not to laugh.'

The Stewart family's lives were abruptly and shockingly disrupted by the Great War in Europe in 1917. America entered the war, and Alex enlisted in October, following in the footsteps of previous Stewarts. 'My father went off to fight in the war in Europe when I was approximately ten years old,' he said. The entire family travelled to New York to see him off. We climbed the Statue of Liberty. To demonstrate my bravery, I attempted to scale the enormous lady's nose... but was stopped. I wasn't so much trying to show that I wasn't afraid of heights as I was trying not to express how afraid I was for my father... and how much I was going to miss him.'I had figured that having my own theatre would be a nice way to keep myself entertained while he was abroad. So, before he left, I told him I wanted to build a theatre in our basement and asked if I could borrow some wooden boards from the store to construct a stage. So he urged Mom to give me what I needed.And he went to fight... and I felt alone... not in a nice manner... not in the way I preferred... Without him, I felt lonely. The house felt deserted. So I started working on my theatre, and with the help of my pals, we created a proscenium, as well as lights and curtains... It was something I really enjoyed. My first work, To Hell with the Kaiser, was a sort of remake of Beat the Kaiser. The second production was more complex than the first. It costs nothing to see it. Mom had to pay as well.

'The Slacker 'was my next project. Looking back, I suppose I was already becoming a conservative... or just a young patriot. In any case, the story is about a man who refuses to fight in the war. Finally, he realises it is his responsibility to fight... and he wins the battle entirely on his own. I played the lead... it was my theatre, therefore I felt comfortable doing so. However, I felt the play had something significant to communicate. What captivated me and my buddies was the task of making it appear as if a combat was taking place. Perhaps simplistic, but we had the footlights flicker to create the effect of shells exploding and red lights to generate the illusion of fires. I was so fascinated in technology that I might have easily become a special-effects designer or art director in movies instead of an actor. But the most important thing about me was that I was completely immersed in everything I did. I believe in the adage, "If it's worth doing, it's worth doing well," so it wasn't a case of me realising I wanted to be an actress. I just wanted to make sure I did it correctly... or as well as I could.'Dad was in Ordnance, which I knew kept him far safer than the guys fighting in the trenches. I never thought he'd be killed... maybe because I thought it only happened to other boys' fathers... or because I thought Dad was such a decent churchgoing man that God wouldn't let anything happen to him. So I was never worried about him.'It's amazing how powerful a simple faith in God can be. God is not going to protect your father simply because you have faith. Simply put, having faith removes your fear. I know this because of the tragic loss of my son [Ronald] in Vietnam. God simply cannot protect every decent soldier. It simply does not operate that way. You can only try to do your best in this life... and faith that something better awaits all of us. That, I suppose, is what true faith is.'

The theatre was closed when his father returned home.

Chapter 3: Education and Inventions

The infant who was born with a "good round shape" grew at what would be considered a normal rate. But once adolescence arrived, the transformation was dramatic: 'I was just a normal-looking kid till I was thirteen. Then I suddenly sprang up... and got thinner at the same time. My parents were worried since they had to continuously buy me new outfits to fit me. Before I was fourteen, I had three new suits. After that, I grew a couple more inches, but they never purchased me a fourth suit. I had to settle for the third suit, which had sleeves that didn't cover my wrists and slacks that came up just short of my ankles.My father and grandfather were both tall, so my height came as no surprise. No one in our family was that slim. Mom became quite concerned about this and had me eat massive amounts of oatmeal every morning. It didn't make me gain weight, but it did make me dislike oatmeal so much that I haven't eaten it since.'Being skinny has been an issue for me at times in my life. I suppose all adolescent guys feel self-conscious, but I had a legitimate reason to be. I decided that no one would ever glance at my legs, so I avoided putting on a bathing suit. People began to suspect I had a fear of water. My only fear was displaying my tiny legs. Oh, that was an issue I had for the majority of my life.'

Jim was free to experiment with whatever tools, materials, and gadgets were available because he spent so much time at his father's merchandise business, and before long he was building fairly advanced technical appliances. 'Jim was no slouch,' Henry Fonda, Jim's adult best buddy, claimed. He was gifted in technological areas. He was never particularly bright intellectually, but he could manufacture stuff. He told me he built a crystal radio when he was twelve. He claimed to have done it with oatmeal boxes and cables. I didn't trust him, so he made a one--and it worked.'

However, as Henry Fonda pointed out, he was not academically accomplished, and his school grades were terrible. 'Simply had a really bad day at school,' Jim explained. 'I wasn't sure if I was just stupid or what. When I was fourteen, I got scarlet fever [which turned into a kidney illness] and had to miss a lot of school. I was out of school for three or four months, which put me behind. My parents hoped that my poor grades were due to those months away from school... but I never did well.'

When the opportunity to fly in an aeroplane arose, Jim, endowed with his father's love of adventure, literally took off to explore a whole new dimension to his life: 'I took my first flight when I was, oh, fourteen or fifteen. It was in a plane piloted by a man named Jack Law, who had served as a pilot in the war. And, like many other pilots who had no other means to make a living after being discharged, they began what was known as barnstorming. These incredible aerobatics would be executed in the air by these pilots in those ancient biplanes. They'd come to town on occasion, and folks might pay for a ride. For fifteen bucks, you get fifteen minutes in the air.

'Wall, I'd been working around the store for a while, saving every nickel I got in the hopes of one day being able to purchase a plane journey. Then we learned that Jack Law was on his way to us.

'My parents were mortified because they thought planes were the riskiest method to travel, and they attempted to persuade me not to fly up... they prohibited me from going up. Some barnstormers had been killed... but only while doing stunts. But I'd made up my mind, and Dad could see, so he questioned almost every client if they'd ever flown in a plane, and some of them had, and none of them had been in a crash, and no one knew of anyone who'd died while going up in a plane, and that kind of calmed him... a little.I couldn't run quickly enough to get to the plane, which was in a nearby field. Dad drove out to the field... but on the way, he stopped to pick up the doctor in case I needed medical attention.'So I took my first flight...

and it was love at first sight. I'd never had anything like it before. I never found anything that could compare to the sensation I'd been having in my dreams. It was more than just freedom. It was the ultimate feeling of being in control... and alone. I've always been an outcast. I don't like being alone, but I do like being alone. Being alone gives me a sense of freedom. And being up there was the most alone I'd ever been. I was flying. It was pure euphoria. 'I simply... it's so difficult to convey... but it's like knowing a little bit what it must be like to be God.' I have no fear of flying and have never had the fear that other people have. I'm terrified of driving, but not of flying. Dad, on the other hand, was not taking any chances. He waited in his car the entire time, with the engine running... just in case he needed to step on it and bring the doctor to the crash site!'

The jet obviously did not crash, and Jim was captivated. But he didn't dare to imagine himself learning to fly a jet one day. He did, however, continue to construct and even invent other contraptions.

Alex encouraged Jim to enjoy such frivolities in life, but he also ensured that his son had more profound and serious experiences-- even if Bessie was against it. 'When President [Warren] Harding died [in August, 1923], I went with my father to the Blairsville Intersection, which was approximately twenty miles distant, where the funeral train would pass,' Jim recounted. We had to leave early in the morning because the train was scheduled to arrive at 3.30 a.m. Mom had said I couldn't go, but around 2.30 a.m. "Come on, Jim," Dad said, waking me up. We'll watch the President's funeral train." I can't think of another time when both Dad and I disobeyed Mom.

Now that Jim was older, and despite his struggles in school, it was clear to him that his father expected certain things from him, such as attending the schools Alex had attended and eventually owning the store. While Jim had little or no say in the schools he attended, he did find a way to indicate to his father that he did not want to own a store.

'As I grew older, Dad definitely expected me to be interested in the store. He thought it was natural for me to take over the store from him. But I was simply uninterested. Dad wanted me to work at the store when I was thirteen to earn my own spending money during the summer vacation. But I told him I didn't want to waste my vacation shopping. That surprised him, and he said, "You've got to do something." "What do you intend to do?" And that's what I said: "I'd like to run the movies in a movie theatre." I liked the idea of spending the summer watching movies, so Dad talked to the owner of the local theatre, and I got the position.'

Alex was able to persuade Jim to attend Mercersburg Academy. 'My father was not prepared for me to attend any high school other than Mercersburg Academy, where Dad had gone, and it was an object lesson in "it's not what you know, it's who you know," Jim remembered. Mercersburg had no intention of admitting me because of my poor academic performance. So Dad went to work on his Presbyterian Church ties, and Mom went to work on her family connections... and before I knew it, I was walking the corridors of Mercersburg. Wall, I didn't do any better than before, and my grades were just... horrible... shameful.'

The school placed a major focus on religion, despite the fact that it was solely open to white Christian males. The same was true at Princeton University, where Jim eventually enrolled; Princeton was unquestionably one of the more upper-class American campuses, with many of its students hailing from some of the East's wealthiest families.

Woody Strode, the black American actor who co-starred with Jim in The Man Who Shot Liberty Valance, stated that he recognized racial characteristics in Stewart and attributed them to Jim's schooling. 'Jimmy Stewart went to schools that were only for white people,' he informed me. They were indoctrinated to worship God and to despise anyone with skin colour darker than theirs. I don't believe the institutions intentionally preached hatred of the black man, but they certainly ingrained bigotry, and I'm sure many Ku Klux Klansmen attended them. Jimmy's entire childhood--his schools, his hometown of Indiana--instilled racism in him and all of his contemporaries. Jimmy deserves credit for not turning out to be a hard-case racist because he is far too wonderful a person to be that way. But he was never at ease around people of colour.'

'It's true that Negroes were excluded from the school, but so were women, and I wasn't brought up to detest women,' Stewart said. Jews were likewise excluded, as were most Indians, while some of our Native Americans were accepted... Although, it must be noted, not many got in.I would agree that my upbringing had an impact on my worldview because I spent so much of my childhood in a town where only white people lived... and I didn't have the opportunity to socialise with individuals of different races at school. Those are not my rules. And I was never a racist.'

Woody Strode, on the other hand, claimed that most white people never truly grasped what it meant to be a racist.

If the schools Jim attended instilled a certain prejudice against black Americans, there was also a concerted effort to discourage sex. 'It was banned to bring girls on campus,' Jim recalled. You see, sex was a sin. That's what they said. I couldn't quite believe it... yet that was the rule. We only received sex education from church ministers. "If you find yourself getting urges, hang a portrait of Theodore Roosevelt on the wall, look into his eyes, and say, 'Help me out here, Teddy.'" You know, boys, I don't think of Theodore Roosevelt when I think of sexual misbehaviour, do you?" I had to agree with him, Wall. 'Now, if it was a photo of Clara Bow...'Girls were occasionally formally invited to a college ball. We were all required to wear tuxedos. However, it provided us with the opportunity to dance with a girl. When you're eighteen and get to dance with a girl, you start thinking to yourself, "Help me out here, Teddy." You couldn't get any closer than that.

'I used to be a fairly excellent dancer. I'd learned some pretty fancy movements, which the girls appreciated. I don't mind revealing that I had girls lining up to dance with me... and the other fellas... Well, they just didn't like it. But the more girls I danced with, the more I turned to Teddy for ideas.'

When inspiration failed to materialise, Jim devised a method of circumventing the rules: 'Wall... It was a little like attempting to escape from Colditz, except you went to the men's room and the girl went to the girls' room--or the staff room because we didn't have any facilities for women. You'd then sneak out for some fresh air, and a minute later the girl would walk out for some fresh air... and you'd meet in a peaceful area, getting no support from Teddy Roosevelt at all. I have to tell you, I had a great time. I was a young man... just an ordinary Joe... and a typical Joe likes to kiss a female.'

Despite the risk of committing carnal sin, Jim reasoned that the school's religious sex guidelines were overly severe. 'As far as I know, the Bible says nothing about "Thou shalt not kiss a girl,"' he says. "Isn't the first commandment in the Bible to be fruitful and multiply?" I once asked one of the clergy who gave us so-called sex education. And he got all worked up and exclaimed, "When you have a wife, you can multiply as much as you want." However, not before." So I discovered that the Bible's loophole was that you just had to make sure you didn't multiply.'

Despite his amorous success, Jim struggled to achieve intellectual success: "I just didn't do well in college." I wasn't the worst student there, but I wasn't the finest either. I was far from being competent. I just found all of the subjects... difficult. My accordion playing was the best thing I did. They were delighted to have me join their orchestra. I was also able to draw. I specialised in cartoons of people... caricatures... thus I became the yearbook's art editor for a few years. In fact, I knew I was strong at drawing, and it was at that time that I decided to pursue a career in design... or the Navy.'I made the decision that I was not going to be an actress. I became a member of the campus drama club. The Stony Batter Drama Club was its name. In my debut play, called The Wolves, I played a French revolutionary. I had to wear baggy trousers that reached my knees. Everyone else was dressed in skintight pants and stockings. Because of my tiny legs, the director thought I looked stupid in tight pants... which I had to agree with... thus I got the part that didn't require tight pants.'I didn't believe I did badly. But the director dismissed me as the clumsiest actor he'd ever had the misfortune to work with. I wasn't very clumsy. Because I was so much taller than everyone else on stage, I just looked ungainly. I was already more than six feet. And being so skinny made me appear even taller. As a result, I felt uneasy on stage. You don't go on stage if you don't want people to look at you.

College life wasn't so horrible. My only significant issue, aside from failing with my studies, was the mocking I received because of my height. And I wasn't done growing! I was also significantly underweight. However, because I was tall, someone thought I'd be ideal for the school [American] football team. As a centre player, I somehow avoided having my ribs cracked for three years. The technique, I discovered, was simple: as soon as you have the ball, get rid of it. They maintained me in the same position for three years since I had a talent for tossing it accurately.

Gloria would subsequently hear all of Jim's life stories at school, and the image he painted for her was far harsher than the one he presented with the public. 'He won't tell you, but he had a hard time at school because of his height and because he talked slowly,' she explained. They started calling him Elmer. Jimmy would tell you it was all in good fun, but as you know, bullies exist at all schools, no matter how prestigious. And there were a few who were critical of

Jimmy. They'd call him Elmer and try to mimic his speech. Jim claims that people have always emulated him, although there were some back then who did it maliciously. What they didn't realise was that Jim had the ability to become really enraged. He's got to learn to control his emotions. Back then, those bullies put him to the test too much, and they went too far--and he just started hitting them until they were all on the floor. He was usually discreet about it. He didn't enjoy it when others knew he was violent. He's deliberately crafted his kind, easygoing image in numerous ways. He never wanted to let anyone down who knew him. He's discovered other ways to express his rage. It does, however, appear on occasion.'

While Jim was learning to control his temper, he was far more successful in learning to control his money. 'I heard all kinds of stories about how tight Jim was with money,' Gloria said. He took a local girl to the movies when he was eighteen or nineteen and home for the holidays. Jim had a lot of money to spend. During the summer, he always worked, either at his father's business or loading bricks for a construction company, and he'd pay for the girl to go to the movies with him. I always assumed he justified the expense so he could kiss the girl in the back row. But after leaving the theatre, they went to a soda shop, and when they sat down, Jim took out a single dime and placed it on the table, saying, "This is what we have to spend, so what'll it be?" Jim might describe it as "frugality." 'Bless him, he's still frugal.'

One of the great historical events that occurred during Jim's adolescence was not something he was directly involved with, but it was an emotional experience for him. When pioneer aviator Charles Lindbergh flew solo from Long Island to Paris, this was the year. 'It happened on May 20, 1927... on my nineteenth birthday,' Jim explained. There was a lot of enthusiasm at the school because the builder of Lindbergh's plane, The Spirit of St. Louis, was Benjamin Franklin Mahoney, a Mercersburg graduate from 1918.

Jim began to feel the burden of impending failure as his Mercersburg graduation date approached. It would undoubtedly disappoint him, but it would also disappoint his parents:

'I barely squeaked by in most of my subjects, but I tanked in Latin. I was able to take an extra exam that would allow me to graduate, so I had to sit for this other Latin exam the night before graduation. My parents had already arrived for graduation the next day, and I knew that failing this exam would have been too humiliating to continue living. But I passed the exam and graduated with my class the next day.' Then I got a surprise for my father. I told him I wanted to attend Annapolis Naval Academy. I expected him to be disappointed because my father was a Princeton man who had always wanted me to attend. He had always thought it was necessary that I follow in his footsteps. And I believe dad truly believed that I would receive the best education possible at Princeton. So it was partly his pride, and partly his desire for me to have the finest. So I was taken aback when he said, "Well, son, let's go take a look at Annapolis," and we drove to the Naval Academy. We took a look around, and I liked what I saw. Then Dad suggested, "Let's take a look at some other places."

Once there, and with his chances of joining the Navy all but gone, Stewart sought an engineering degree and began fantasising about a career in aviation. However, by the conclusion of his first year at Princeton in 1929, he had fallen so far behind in his academics that he needed to attend summer school. His ambitions were once again dashed there.

Chapter 4: The Lady's Gentleman

The stock market fell in 1929, kicking off America's dreadful Depression. 'It felt to me that was the end of both my days at Princeton and my dreams of becoming an architect,' Jim said. I just couldn't see how Dad was going to pay for me to keep on. But Dad was so determined... he took out loans... he had to lay off some of his employees... he worked longer hours himself... simply to keep me in college.'

Jim contributed financially by performing in a touring magic show with his friend Bill Neff. Neff had become a professional magician and was constantly touring from town to town in Pennsylvania. 'I took my accordion along, and whenever we arrived in town, Bill hung himself upside down from a street light or a tree by a rope around his ankle, and I stood and announced details of the night's show, playing my accordion for added emphasis,' Jim remembered.

Joshua Logan was a Princeton student. He played football, boxed, and was involved in school drama, where he refined abilities that would help him carve out a successful career as a director on Broadway and in Hollywood. He would also play a role in shaping the careers of James Stewart and Henry Fonda. 'I met Jim through the Triangle Club, which put on various plays and shows at the university,' Logan explained. Jim got interested because he was a fantastic accordionist. That was his strongest suit. He was also a great guy, but we truly respected him for his accordion playing. We didn't know anyone else who could play the accordion, and it was a great instrument to have because you could easily transport it on and off stage. So, when we were working on The Golden Dog and needed a musical interlude, we asked Jim to do it. He was such a hit and such a delightful guy to have around that he appeared in a number of additional performances, always just showing up to play his accordion to ecstatic acclaim.

Jose Ferrer, who, like Jim, had planned a career as an architect until he discovered acting at Princeton, was another student who knew Stewart well. He was also a blossoming musician, like Jim. 'James Stewart stood out from the crowd because of his accordion,' he explained. We were both members of the Charter Club. There are numerous clubs available at universities. Then there were the more opulent and prestigious clubs--and then there was the Charter Club. Music was our main focus in Charter. Stewart had his accordion, and I had a dancing band. We also shared a desire to be architects, so we had something in common. But it was music that brought us together.

Jim also did well with the girls, even if they were with another young man. And, according to Joshua Logan, he did it all with ease: 'When it came to girls, Jim was never the bashful guy people would believe he was. Even back then, it was easy to assume he was shy among girls and naïve. That was his approach to women. At gatherings, any Princeton student had to keep an eye out for him. No matter how attractive you were, if your girl fell for Jimmy Stewart's way of looking and acting like a backwoods hick, you'd find her dancing with Jimmy or fleeing into the moonlight on his arm. He was too much for the girl. And I believe he quickly realised that he didn't have to make much of an effort to pick up girls. They were drawn to him.

'One night, a man attempted to assault Jimmy because his girlfriend had deserted him in favour of Jim. Jimmy just stood there, all innocent, saying, "Look, I didn't mean to steal your girl." She's right here. It's fine if she wants to accompany you. But what can I do if she decides she wants to stay with me?" And when this guy tried to deliver a right punch, Jimmy simply sidestepped to the left, kept his right foot where it was, and tripped him up. "Golly, are you all right?" Jimmy assisted him up. Did you injure yourself?" And he seemed to have done nothing, and everyone thought the other person deserved what he got. Jimmy also got the girl. The way Jimmy obtained his females was an art form.'

Jim and Logan frequently performed musical performances on the Triangle Club's annual Christmas tour of many cities. 'It was kinda fun,' Jim added, 'since it was a free way to get down to New York and other big places. There were 75 of us being moved, and it was a really pleasant experience.'

'What Jimmy won't tell you is that the tour was always a terrific means of meeting women,' Joshua Logan recalled. Girls assumed we were celebrities, which is an easy method to get girls interested in you. On these trips, Jimmy was less predatory because if you stole another fella's female, you had to suffer with the penalties for the remainder of the tour. But the females were smitten by Jimmy. I had no idea how many girls he had to leave behind. Not that we were all blameless. It's simply that when most people think of Jimmy Stewart, they don't think of him as a ladies' guy. 'However, the girls adored him.'

Things wouldn't change when he arrived in Hollywood, where he would become the object of desire for some of the industry's most gorgeous female stars. But it was actress Margaret Sullavan who captured Jim's heart for years--some say all his life, or at least until Gloria came along.

'I first met Margaret Sullavan when she was in a travelling production of The Artist and the Lady, and the play came to Princeton... and I was the stage manager,' Jim recounted. I thought she was a really nice girl... and our friendship continued... till she died.'

Like many others who knew Jim and Margaret Sullavan well, Joshua Logan maintained that Jim and Sullavan loved each other from the beginning: 'There was much more to the friendship. It was there from the start, when she arrived at Princeton with a play. He was head over heels in love with her. He was so taken with her that he invited her to a Charter Club reception. Sullavan said it was the longest, slowest, shyest, but most genuine invitation she'd ever gotten from a man, and she fell for him as well. They had been in love since the beginning.' 'I always knew he was deeply in love with Margaret Sullavan, and she was with him,' Gloria said of Jim and Sullavan's affair, which lasted long into their Hollywood careers. But she was more enamoured with her job.'

Jim accepted every invitation to participate with his trusty accordion in Triangle productions, whether he was aiming for a career on stage or simply enjoyed playing his accordion in front of an audience. 'Jim got requested to act in all those Triangle plays purely because they loved the notion of having someone on stage who could play a portable instrument,' Logan explained. Spanish Blades was a satire about Don Juan and Don Quixote in which Jim played a troubadour who travelled throughout Spain playing... his accordion.'

But before long, he was taking parts in shows that didn't require him to play the accordion. He played a butler in The Play's the Thing, and a 'modern proletarian' in Nerissa, as Jim called it. 'The college reviewers agreed that I made a better butler than a proletariat, but they liked my musicianship in Spanish Blade to my acting in either play. So there was no motivation to become an actress.'

Jim maintained he had no real interest in becoming a professional actor, and in explaining how he found himself getting involved in the theatre, he neglected to mention that Margaret Sullavan had a great deal to do with his decision to join Logan's company: 'I never intended on doing another play after Nerissa. It was a dark period. The Depression rendered work prospects bleak. I was lucky because I had a scholarship for my Masters studies, so I had something to go on with. But I was really beginning to question where my future lay. And then I heard the news that Charles Lindbergh's infant child had been kidnapped. It was something that happened not far from Princeton, so everybody was talking about it. And Lindbergh was kind of my hero, and I felt so desperate . . . so horrible for him. I could only guess how Lindbergh must have felt when they discovered the lifeless body of his son. That tragedy significantly coloured my life at that time.

'The trouble for Jim was that by the time he arrived in West Falmouth, Margaret Sullavan had left us to return to Broadway, where she was a growing star,' Logan stated. She was already a well-known talent before joining the University Players. All of our players were there only for the sake of having fun. Another budding theatre star in our group was Henry Fonda. And he and Sullavan fell in love, and they married on Christmas Day, 1931.Fonda and Sullavan had known one another for a few years and had worked together in plays. He first despised her. Fonda had nothing good to say about her when they arrived on Cape Cod. But, like many others, he succumbed to her charm. She has the potential to be a genuine sassy. She was also a lot of fun and quite passionate. Fonda was won over by the fun and sensuality, and he married her.Jim was devastated by everything. He knew Sullavan had left us before he arrived, which was a huge disappointment. Then he found out she'd married Fonda, which, I believe, crushed his heart. He wasn't the type of guy who would begrudge Fonda for marrying the lady he adored, and when they met that summer, he and Fonda became the best of friends. Furthermore, Sullavan and Fonda divorced just a few months after their marriage, and she began having affairs with other men--important Broadway guys. Fonda returned to us in the summer. Jim was aware of everything before he came out to join us. Being on stage, or whether he simply enjoyed playing his accordion in front of a crowd, Jim embraced every chance to appear in Triangle shows with his faithful instrument. 'Jim got requested to act in all those Triangle plays purely because they loved the notion of having someone on stage who could play a portable instrument,' Logan explained. Spanish

Blades was a satire about Don Juan and Don Quixote in which Jim played a troubadour who travelled throughout Spain playing... his accordion.'

But before long, he was taking parts in shows that didn't require him to play the accordion. He played a butler in The Play's the Thing, and a 'modern proletarian' in Nerissa, as Jim called it. 'The college reviewers agreed that I made a better butler than a proletariat, but they liked my musicianship in Spanish Blade to my acting in either play. So there was no motivation to become an actress.'

Jim maintained that he had no desire to become a professional actor, and in explaining how he became involved in the theatre, he failed to mention that Margaret Sullavan had a large influence on his decision to join Logan's company: 'I never intended on doing another play after Nerissa. It was a dark period. The Depression harmed job opportunities. I was fortunate to have a scholarship for my Masters studies, so I could continue my education. But I was beginning to think about my future. Then I learned that Charles Lindbergh's baby boy had been abducted. Everyone was talking about it because it happened not far from Princeton. And Lindbergh was a hero of mine, and I felt terrible... so bad for him. I couldn't help but imagine how Lindbergh felt when they discovered his son's body. That tragedy had a significant impact on my life at the time.

'The trouble for Jim was that by the time he arrived in West Falmouth, Margaret Sullavan had left us to return to Broadway, where she was a growing star,' Logan stated. She was already a well-known talent before joining the University Players. All of our players were there only for the sake of having fun. Another budding theatre star in our group was Henry Fonda. And he and Sullavan fell in love, and they married on Christmas Day, 1931.Fonda and Sullavan had known one another for a few years and had worked together in plays. He first despised her. Fonda had nothing good to say about her when they arrived on Cape Cod. But, like many others, he succumbed to her charm. She has the potential to be a genuine sassy. She was also a lot of fun and quite passionate. Fonda was won over by the fun and sensuality, and he married her. Jim was devastated by everything. He knew Sullavan had left us before he arrived, which was a huge disappointment. Then he found out she'd married Fonda, which, I believe, crushed his heart. He wasn't the type of guy who would begrudge Fonda for marrying the lady he adored, and when they met that summer, he and Fonda became the best of friends. Besides, Sullavan and Fonda divorced just a few months after their marriage, and she began having affairs with other men--important Broadway men--before returning to us in the summer. Jim was aware of everything before he came out to join us. 'But he still came.'

Chapter 5: Taking the Center Stage

'I arrived at the Falmouth Theatre on Old Silver Beach with my accordion, and I began playing in the tearoom,' Jim remembered of his first day on Cape Cod. Before and after each act, I was meant to entertain the audience. Maybe I was playing the incorrect songs, because I was dismissed after customers complained that my music gave them heartburn.'

That story appeared to be one of Jim's slightly taller-than-average fables. 'According to Jim, he was dismissed after the first evening,' Logan added. In reality, he was never dismissed. He spent the entire summer playing his accordion. He also worked as an usher in the theatre. I kept in touch with Sullavan on a regular basis, and Jim was always interested in hearing about her. I wondered whether that was what kept him at Cape Cod during the summer of 1932.'

'I took one look at the Falmouth Theatre on Old Silver Beach... and I guess I had my first thought that I might just want to be an actor after all,' Jim remarked, referring to the architect in him. It was a stunning structure. A beautiful building, I believe, can have the same effect as a beautiful lady. You see it--or she--and you want to be there. Perhaps it was my architect's vision that drew me to that location. 'However, I knew I wanted to be there.'

His connection with Henry Fonda began there. 'My friendship with Fonda dates back 47 years,' Jim stated in 1979. It began in 1932. I'd recently graduated from college. He'd been an actor for a few years before me. I began in a stock company where he had worked for numerous years.

'I was never a broke actor. Fonda was a striving young actor. He claimed I just happened to be in the right place at the right time. But there was never any doubt in Fonda's mind about what he wanted to do. I just graduated from college... I was going to be an architect...

but acting bites you like a mosquito... because you get bit. It becomes a full-fledged thing.'

'I just liked him,' Fonda said of his early acquaintance with Jim. He had nothing to dislike about him. He had a beautiful yet modest sense of comedy that drew me in. He made me laugh, and I think I made him laugh as well. It's impossible to pin down what makes two people click so well. But we clicked--and continued clicking--for years. We were and still are quite different people. Our political perspectives are virtually diametrically opposed. Jim has a different type of private life than I do. My life has been somewhat chaotic, whereas Jim's has been fairly stable since he married Gloria. But he's never chastised me for my errors, and he's never lectured me. He's only there when I need him. What more could you ask for in a friend? And he got me interested in creating model aeroplanes. That is a shared interest of ours. We spend hours assembling these miniature aeroplanes. Like a couple of children. I couldn't live without that companionship.'

However, during the Communist witch-hunts of 1947, their friendship was unable to withstand their opposing political views--and Fonda's distaste for the position Jim would put himself in by agreeing to work for J Edgar Hoover, Director of the FBI, in the right-wing quest to catch Hollywood's Communists, caused a long-term rift. Jim's love for Margaret Sullavan, on the other hand, was unbreakable.

When I met Fonda in 1976, he made no mention of Jim's passion for Sullavan, despite the fact that, according to Joshua Logan and others, Fonda was aware of it. What people liked about Jim was that he didn't disturb everyone with his grief at losing Sullavan, whereas Fonda would tell everyone how miserable he was. 'Hank moaned about Margaret all the time, but Jim kept his thoughts to himself,' Logan explained. I kept Jim busy so he wouldn't waste time lamenting his missed opportunity [with Sullavan]. He worked in the tearooms, was an usher, and helped build the sets. He also had minor roles in theatre. I could tell he was serious about acting. He regarded it as a skill that he needed to learn--and that he could learn. He started working on techniques. I could tell he was enjoying himself.'

When it came to acting, there were two things that irritated Jim the most. The first was that acting was an art, and the second was that Jim's acting technique was simply a natural extension of his personality. 'You have to approach acting as a craft, not as an art,' he remarked. And the only way to learn is to practise. I know a lot of people go to acting schools and a few of them become successful... but you don't have to. People who are good performers when they leave those schools are good when they enter. They already have the skill. All they need is the ability... and the ability can only be obtained by working as an actor. It's not taught in any acting school. It's something you learn on stage... working with other actors... and directors... and in front of an audience. You figure out what works and what doesn't. You discover what you're doing incorrectly and what you're doing correctly. It's a skill, not a bizarre faith. To be an actor, you do not need to meditate. It's like any other craft... like carpentry or building... you may have the talent, but you have to do it to do it correctly.

Even though he had some acting talent to begin with, Jim spent years honing his craft. And he had something else that appeared to be his biggest flaw at first, something that may prohibit him from ever being a successful actor-his looks.

Logan claimed that if Margaret Sullavan had stayed, Jim would have found it difficult to have a relationship with her because he was so preoccupied with perfecting his acting technique. 'There was really no time for ladies,' Logan explained. 'We were all too preoccupied for that.' 'We all had our fun, if we wanted it,' Henry Fonda recalled. You could immerse yourself in work and take cold showers if you wanted to. Jim probably thought he'd died and gone to heaven because he'd spent most of his time at university with males. But here he was, surrounded by men and women. There was a cottage for all of the males and another for all of the women. After a long day's work, I'm sure a lot of the employees just wanted to sleep. But we were only kids, for Christ's sake, and you only needed an hour or so after work to have some fun with some chick.

'I admired a girl there called Cynthia Rogers,' Jim admitted, recalling spending time with several of the actresses. She worked as an actress. We were all quite young. Life was lovely.'

Life continued to be enjoyable for Jim, but there appeared to be little light at the end of the Cape Cod tunnel for Fonda as an actor. So he left the University Players and went to work as a backstage hand for a small theatre group in Maine. 'I carried on failing as an actor, largely because I wasn't acting, but Jim-Lucky Jim-stayed on and got a shortcut to Broadway!' he recounted.

In 1932, Jim received both good and bad news. Jim's grandfather, James Maitland Stewart, died at the age of 91. Despite his rather nasty demeanour in old age, he had remained a respected member of the Indiana community. The mayor and other significant local civil and political officials were among the pallbearers when he died.

The good news was that Joshua Logan, Bretaigne Windust, and Charles Crane Leatherbee had struck a deal with New York producer Arthur J Beckhard, which Hank Fonda had missed out on. He had agreed to try out a number of plays with the University Players in Cape Cod in August before producing them in New York.

The first of Beckhard's pieces began rehearsing with the Theatre Unit after the touring group had left. But there were issues from the start. 'The first play was Goodbye Again [a comedy by Allan Scott and George Haight], but Beckhard offered the main character to Howard Lindsay, an actor who wasn't in our group,' Logan explained. That didn't go over well. Bretaigne Windust directed the play and ensured that certain of our players, including Jimmy Stewart, had roles.'

Jim's contribution was little. 'I played a chauffeur who came on--the set was a famous author's home--and I carried a book which I presented to the author's butler and I said, "Mrs Belle Irving would surely appreciate it if she could have this book autographed," he recounted. The butler left, returned, and stated that the author was too busy to autograph the book. "Mrs Belle Irving is going to be sore as hell," I muttered as I exited. I was immediately captivated by the notion of bringing two simple lines to life. That's what makes acting so fascinating.'

Despite the behind-the-scenes squabbles, which Jim avoided, Beckhard chose to bring Carry Nation to Broadway in September 1932. The producer wanted to bring the Cape Cod production's cast and staff to New York to save money and time. 'I was meant to be in the University Players for only the summer... and suddenly there was this possibility to play on Broadway,' Jim realised. My parents, on the other hand, expected me to return to Princeton. 'As a result, I had to think carefully about what to do.' I simply imagined how wonderful it would be to perform on a Broadway stage. This was something that all the other performers desired, and I thought I was a lucky guy to have it delivered to me on a silver platter. So I devised every excuse I could think of to avoid returning to Princeton. Dad was displeased. I told him he'd already spent too much money on my sisters. Mary was going to Carnegie Tech to study art, whereas Virginia was going to Vassar. I explained to Dad that I would just be another cost he couldn't afford. "Son, your tuition is free," he said. You received a scholarship." I went on to say, "But I need to be able to feed myself." "Don't worry about it," Dad said. We'll make it." I eventually had to inform my parents that I was leaving for New York. They were displeased. I never imagined I'd make it as an actor. I simply went along for the ride since possibilities kept coming my way.'

Virginia, Jim's sister, was in New York at the time. Gloria compared Virgina--or Ginnie--to Jim rather than Dotie. She was laid-back and even resembled him. She was also a daydreamer who became easily distracted; she did not complete her freshman year at Vassar. But she was Bessie's favourite of the three kids, and the one Mother lavished the most attention on.

Virginia aspired to be a writer, and in February 1940, she had an article titled 'My Brother Becomes a Star' published in the Coronet. She wrote of meeting Jim following the failure of Carry Nation and sharing a Thanksgiving meal in a restaurant.

The drama premiered on December 28th at the Masque Theatre. It was a big success, lasting six months. Burgess Meredith saw the performance and recalls Stewart's ability to squeeze every drop of juice from his two lines: 'Jim was simply magnificent in bringing out so much from two lines. Imagine a tall, lanky man wearing this hideous chauffeur's attire, looking perplexed and befuddled. Then he says, "Mrs Irving would sure..." Jim extended the word "sure" to become "surrre..." He sounded like he was stuck on "r." Then he's left on stage alone. Any actor enjoys having the stage to himself, except Jim, who has nothing to say. So he just stands there, embarrassed and befuddled, and the audience loves it. The butler then reappears, says "No," and Jim does another long drawn out "r" with the word "sore." And then he says "hell"... and his delivery of that phrase is so fantastic that the audience roars with laughter every time. This was an actor who could take two lines and turn them into the play's highlight in ways the creator could never have predicted.'

Around that time, Henry Fonda came to New York, unemployed, and moved in with Jim, Logan, and McCormick. 'I was out of work more often than Jim, and I'd been performing since 1925,' Henry Fonda recounted. He'd been doing it for several months. That's why I gave him the nickname Lucky Jim.'

They all survived by spreading the cost as thinly as possible. 'We had a general fund that we all contributed money into, which was there for the leaner times... when we'd all be out of work,' Jim recounted. Otherwise, it was always the fella... or fellas who worked the hardest who carried the most financial load.

In addition to whining about a lack of work, Henry Fonda also moaned about his divorce from Margaret Sullavan. 'Jimmy had to listen to Hank moaning about Sullavan,' Logan recounted. And Jimmy attentively listened to everything. Hank may have attempted to discourage Jim from trying his luck with Sullavan because the divorce of Fonda and Sullavan was finalised in 1933.

Jim recalled, 'Gangsters managed the prostitution operation, and the prostitutes had a lot of clientele in the block where we resided.' Which begs the question: did Stewart and Fonda take advantage of the prostitutes' services? Logan, who had moved out but still stayed over when he was in New York, stated, 'There's no doubt. These were men. These were grown males. These were young lads with a bachelor pad, where there was little else to do but drink and... mess around with chicks. "Let's hire ourselves some hookers," Hank would offer, and Jim would always be the more hesitant. I believe he always assumed that some Presbyterian spy would find him out, and I believe he felt guilty to some measure because he had a religious strain on him. However, he only felt guilty after the... incident. And he gradually felt less guilty. He went on to say, "We all need redeeming, Josh, and the more you fall, the better your redeeming." Jim practised his redemption for years.'

'We couldn't afford 'em,' Jim said of hiring hookers. We'd frequently return home to discover our apartment locked because we hadn't paid the rent. So you scraped together enough money to pay the rent and then ate as cheaply as possible. If you had some money, you went out and got some alcohol.'

Fonda, on the other hand, had a different take on their impoverished living. 'With gangsters everywhere, it wasn't difficult to find some tax-free labour. Nothing major. We didn't knock anyone down. But we kept an eye on the gals... the hookers... from time to time. The problem was that hookers frequently desired protection from these hoodlums, but they didn't want to pay up their hard-earned money. So we'd let them hide out from time to time... and they'd demonstrate their appreciation in more personal ways.'

When I questioned if that meant using the girls' professional services, Fonda smiled and answered, 'Yeah!' Without a doubt! When a nice-looking female offers you a good time and you don't have anything else to do, you don't answer, "No thanks, not today." As a result, we'd have some girls to ourselves. Normally, Myron would refuse to participate and would leave. He could be heard saying, "I don't want to be here if those gangsters come barging in and find their girls giving us freebies." Josh did not live with us all of the time. So Jim had a girl in one room, and I had a girl in another.'And, yes, we were caught one night. The gangsters barged in and apprehended Jim and me with the girls. Either get beaten up or pay up. Jim resolved to be a hero. He can get incredibly angry, and when he does, he may be terrifying. But there was also some acting involved. He assured them he wasn't frightened of them, and if they tried anything on him, he'd show them what it meant to mess with... some name he made up for himself... something like "The Pennsylvanian Kid." I assumed they'd simply shoot him. But they merely looked at each other, shrugged, murmured, "Have a good time," and walked away.Jim told me, "Don't ever let me do that again." And because he pretended to be tough, they assigned us a few other little assignments.'

'One night... A dead body was discovered in front of our building. Gangsters had shot him. He was most likely a gangster himself. But nothing seemed real to us. We were in our own world, figuring out how to make it in the theatre business.'I frequently wished I could have done more to aid in the fight against crime. I believe I would have enjoyed working for the FBI. I've always appreciated the FBI's job... and I admired and liked J Edgar Hoover.'

In the years since, Stewart has not only played a role in the fight against crime, but he has come as close to being an FBI agent as someone can without wearing a badge or receiving a salary from the federal government. He'd also made friends with J Edgar Hoover.

'For years, Jim nearly idolised Hoover, and he thought the FBI was the greatest law enforcement outfit in the world,' Fonda added. He never changed his mind about working with the FBI. He'd go on and on about how Hoover had cleaned up America by apprehending gangsters such as Pretty Boy Floyd, John Dillinger, and Baby Face Nelson.' Jim, on the other hand, would change his opinion regarding Hoover. However, this occurred only after Hoover's death in 1972.

'By 1933, we were able to afford to rent a speakeasy on West 40th Street every Thursday where we and other like-minded performers congregated,' Fonda says. The Thursday Night Beer Club was our moniker. We charged $2 for a beverage and a steak, which I generally prepared. Jim's role was to perform the music and arrange for other musicians to appear. Then news got to the professional musicians who were performing on the radio or in hotels and theatres, and they started showing up.'

Burgess Meredith was a frequent visitor. He was struggling as a musician at the time before resorting to acting. 'We had some wonderful nights,' he said. It quickly became the place to be. There were prominent musicians like Benny Goodman in attendance, as well as actresses like Ruth Gordon, Helen Hayes, and Margaret Sullavan.Sullavan adored Jim, and vice versa. It should have been that simple. But they did nothing about it. Part of the reason, I believe, was Jim's desire not to offend Fonda. But it was clear to everyone that Sullavan adored Jim. 'She genuinely handled Jim differently than she did other men. She didn't pay much attention to men unless she was sexually interested in them. You could tell when Sullavan was interested in you, and few men could stand up to her because she was so cunning when it came to seduction. But she was merely affectionate with Jim, not predatory. She appeared to want to protect him, nurture him, and help him become everything he could be. I believe Jim made it apparent to her at some time that, while he loved her--and I mean, he was in love with her--they would never be lovers, and I believe this had everything to do with his friendship with Henry Fonda. I don't know what other man she would have accepted it from, but she took it from Jimmy, and she never ceased being affectionate and even maternal towards him. She abruptly claimed one night that Jimmy was going to become a great movie star. She had recently secured a contract with Universal Studios.'

Joshua Logan wasn't certain Jim had what it required to be a movie star at the time. 'I think it's possible that Margaret was promoting Jimmy Stewart as a future star solely to get at Fonda,' he said, implying that Sullavan was doubtful.

Anthony Mann, Jim's most important director, came into his life briefly during his stay at the rented speakeasy. Jim mainly avoided inquiries about Mann because of a schism in their friendship that happened in 1957, but he did tell me, 'The first time I met Anthony Mann was when he started showing up to what we dubbed our Thursday Night Beer Club. But his name wasn't Tony Mann back then. Emil Bundsmann was there, and he wasn't a director. He worked as a stage manager. He went on to direct some plays in New York, I believe.' Anthony Mann would have a significant impact on Jim's film career; he was the man who made Jim renowned as a Western actor.

Jim had become friends with actress Jane Cowl, one of the greatest Juliets of the American stage. Cowl was in her late forties, but she exuded grace and confidence. 'There was nothing romantic between Jim and Jane Cowl,' said Burgess Meredith, 'but nearly every woman who met Jim seemed to love him, and I think Jane Cowl did.'

Cowl was set to play Camille in Boston in the spring of 1933, and when she learned that Goodbye Again had closed, she asked that Jim be employed as Camille's stage manager. This encounter inspired one of Jim's famous stories, which has had several endings throughout the years.

In the autumn of 1933, Jim and Fonda worked together again in the play All Good Americans. 'We weren't exactly taking New York by storm,' Fonda admitted. I was the lead's understudy, and all Jimmy had to do was play his accordion.' 'They simply wanted someone who could play the accordion, and I was it,' Jim recalled. I didn't realise I had a scenario where I had to throw the accordion out the window until I got the job. Wall... I was playing my own accordion, which I wasn't about to throw away. So I persuaded them to let me play the banjo instead of the accordion because banjos are much cheaper.'

Early in 1934, Jim auditioned for the lead part in stage producer Leonard Sillman's New Faces of 1934, a play about Broadway hopefuls. Jim learned that Sillman was staying at the Algonquin Hotel and planned to 'accidentally' run into him in the hotel lobby, where he instantly performed an improvised humorous sketch. 'I've already signed another underweight young comedian,' Sillman told Jim. Henry Fonda was an underweight comedian.

Around the same time, Jim landed an audition for the lead role of Sergeant O'Hara in Sidney Howard's Yellow Jack, a story about how soldiers were used as guinea pigs to test the origins of yellow fever. 'I believed I delivered a solid audition,' Jim recounted. I'd read and studied the play, and I think I impressed the producers. "But can you play the part with an Irish brogue?" they asked. Wall, I tried my hardest, but I just couldn't pull off a remotely convincing Irish brogue. So I asked a friend of mine, Frank Cullinan, a terrific actor and expert at dialects, to teach me how to talk with an Irish brogue. I persuaded the producers to allow me another audition, but the part had already been cast, despite their admiration for my Irish brogue. So I had a new ability to add to my resume: an Irish brogue. However, a few days later, they contacted me to tell me that the actor they'd chosen for O'Hara wasn't working out, and they offered me the job.

Yellow Jack premiered to critical acclaim at the Martin Beck Theatre on March 6, 1934, but the subject was too gloomy to appeal to the general public. After a brief run, McClintic promised Jim a role in Divided by Three, a play about a young man shaken by his mother's adultery that will be produced in the autumn and starring Judith Anderson.

Jim spent the summer playing stock theatre on Long Island, and he even got a small part in Art Troubles, a two-reel comedy starring Shemp Howard of The Three Stooges. 'I didn't think I'd be able to break into movies,' Stewart admitted. 'I was offered the position for $50 per day, which was a lot of money to me at the time, so I just took it as a job.'

Jim came to New York in the autumn of 1934, and he and Fonda settled into the Madison Square Hotel. Fonda was having a successful Broadway run in The Farmer Takes a Wife, and Jim was looking forward to success in Divided by Three. Their Madison Square Hotel apartment was less interesting and risky than the two-room apartment on the third floor of West 64th Street. 'Jim was always in love with aeroplanes and the concept of flying, and his excitement was kind of infectious,' Fonda said. So we began making model planes. We were particularly interested in a Martin Bomber that we were constructing. Our apartment was filled with balsa wood and wood shavings, and it smelled strongly of glue. But before we could finish, I was called to Hollywood to do my first film there, The Farmer Takes a Wife, which I had previously done on Broadway.'

Jim proceeded to work on Divided by Three rehearsals. Hedda Hopper, a B-movie actress at the time, was also in the cast; she eventually quit acting to become a famous Hollywood gossip columnist. She and Stewart struck it up right away, but no one liked leading woman Judith Anderson. She was upset about everything about the play, especially the casting of James Stewart, who was supposed to play her son but was just ten years her junior.

'Anderson was a scary actress--as intimidating as hell,' Henry Fonda recalled after seeing the play. But there was Jim on stage, eye-to-eye with her... and he was just so good. At the end of the performance, I went to his dressing room and simply sat there gazing at him, shaking my head and thinking to myself, "Where the hell did this come from?" "How the hell did he get so good?" I was working my tail off trying to make it as an actor, and here was this guy from Indiana who thought acting was a lark, and he was turning into a star and a darn excellent actor. It ruffled my feathers, to be honest.'

Fonda actually didn't have much to complain about. During his appearance in New Faces of 1934, he was signed by an agent who won him a contract with Hollywood producer Walter Wanger, and so Fonda arrived in Hollywood later that year.

Chapter 6: Hollywood

'Jim would never deny Hopper's assertions that she got him his screen test because after he became a star, she championed him in his profession and in politics, and he was devoted to her for that,' Burgess Meredith said. Jim will never confirm or reject Hopper's claim. That, I believe, tells a lot about Jim's dedication to friendship. He's just the type of guy everyone should have as a friend.'

Additional tests were conducted. Finally, Altman was able to give Jim a typical six-month beginner's contract, with the option of signing him for seven years at $350 per week. Jim signed, but first committed to two more plays: Page Miss Glory, which opened on November 6, 1934, at the Mansfield Theatre, and A Journey by Night, which opened on April 15, 1935, at the Shubert. The second piece was a flop, lasting only seven performances and earning Jim his first negative reviews as a Viennese complete with a horrible Viennese accent. However, by the spring of 1935, James Stewart was prepared to test the waters of Hollywood. 'I was waiting for Jim at the station when he arrived in Los Angeles,' Henry Fonda recounted. I'd been waiting for Jim for hours, but he kept missing trains from New York, so I never knew when he'd come. He finally pulled in. "Where am I going to live?" he asked. "Never mind," I answered. "Where has the Martin Bomber gone?" And there it was, in its own carton. Jim didn't forget it, which surprised me. So I drove him and his luggage to the property I was renting in Brentwood, and he remained with me.

Stewart was never able to meet Garbo in the studio or in the garden. Garbo apparently contributed to the problem by erecting an unusually high fence between their residences. 'Garbo didn't like Hank's cats,' Stewart explained. 'At least, Hank considered them to be his pets. They were essentially ferocious monsters dressed up as cute and cuddly. And because Hank loves cats, he was always leaving food out for them. And boy, did they multiply, so there were more of these wild cats every month. This did not sit well with Garbo, so she erected this high fence to keep the cats out. And maybe it was there to keep us out.'

Jim came to Hollywood weighing just 132 pounds, so they tried fattening him up with pills and sending him to the gym every day to firm his muscles. 'I had a trainer named Don Loomis. He had massive muscles. He had the appearance of Mr. Universe... and he was a taskmaster. I was being pushed to the brink of weariness. I got to press 200 pounds fifty times, and I actually gained 20 pounds and gained muscle. "More, give me more," he urged. Just one more. "There are two more." "I can't do this anymore," I finally said. If you keep putting pressure on me, I'm going to die... and then what will Mr. Mayer think?"

After the Thin Man, the second in what would become a series of films based on Dashiell Hammett's Nick and Nora Charles mysteries, was chosen to introduce Jim to the general audience in a supporting role. Despite the fact that William Powell and Myrna Loy were cast, they were only paid B-movie pay. Loy revolted, and MGM became embroiled in what appeared to be a protracted contract dispute with the actress.

Bill Grady proposed to producer Harry Rapf that he cast Jim in The Murder Man as Shorty, a reporter! 'I think it was the really weird idea that I play a guy named Shorty that convinced the producer that it was just bizarre enough to work,' Jim explained. Spencer Tracy appeared in the 1934 film The Murder Man as a wisecracking newspaperman famed for his scoops on major crime cases who becomes caught in a personal problem when his father goes bankrupt after being duped by two guys. Tracy investigates after one of the con men is found slain, and the surviving con guy is jailed for fraud and murder.

The Murder Man failed to make an impression when it was released in 1935, and Jim's supporting role went unnoticed. 'That's how they worked you,' he explained. 'You could play minor parts in movies, and it didn't matter if they were bad because you weren't the star. So you keep working till they decide whether you have what it takes or not.'

He was soon back on the set of Rose Marie, the second musical film starring Jeanette MacDonald and Nelson Eddy after their success with Naughty Marietta. Jim portrayed the fugitive brother, which he described as "really the best kind of part for me at the time." 'I didn't have many scenes, but everyone speaks about this character, and at the conclusion of the movie, I got my big role. So, even though I didn't have much screen time, my contribution was significant. I had a good time making the picture. We had some location work to do. I shared a room with the film's director, Woody Van Dyke, and he appreciated it when I played the accordion to put him to sleep at night. It was fortunate that he liked me because he likes to accomplish everything in one go to save time and money. But I messed up a few of my scenes, so we had to reshoot them. But he was kind to me and encouraged me to do my best.

Jim jumped right into another film, Next Time We Love, which he was loaning to Universal. He compared contract actors to baseball players. 'You were moved around between studios. Universal wanted to utilise the MGM backlot for three weeks, so MGM agreed if I played a role in their picture.'

According to Ray Milland, one of the film's two primary stars, there was a lot more behind Universal's choice to hire Jim. 'Margaret Sullavan was the star, and she was a big star at Universal, which was not a very big studio at the time, and they did anything she asked them to do. And one of the things she requested was that Jimmy Stewart be cast in Next Time We Love. And Sullavan received what she asked for.'

Jim was listed third, after Sullavan and Milland. He portrayed an international newspaper correspondent who is torn between his own profession and that of his wife (Sullavan), a Broadway actress. However, the marriage is doomed since Sullavan has another lover, played by Milland. Unhappily, Stewart's character dies of an illness in China, leaving Sullavan and Milland to marry.

'Margaret went out of her way to make Jimmy seem good in what I guess was just his third film,' Milland said of Sullavan, who married film director William Wyler in 1934. Our director [Edward Griffith] was furious with Jimmy because of his excessive stage methods, and he could have helped Jimmy if he had been a better director. Margaret, on the other hand, assisted him. Oh, they practised late into the night... and I'm not saying they were having an affair. Jimmy's performance clearly improved as a result of Margaret's teaching. But you just knew these two folks were in love.

When the filming was finished and Jim returned to MGM, he was apparently a "new man," as Gloria phrased it. 'Margaret taught him a lot about screen technique,' she said. He exuded confidence that the studio execs had never seen before. I believe they had already concluded he was going nowhere, but he displayed a new sense of confidence in his next few photos. And Sullavan gave it to him.'

As a result, Margaret Sullavan can be credited with one of Jim's first positive film reviews, from Time, which stated when the film was released in 1936: 'James Stewart is genuine, spontaneous, and altogether terrific.' The film itself was critically panned. 'A draggy, convoluted tale [that] will have to be sold on the star's previous performances,' Variety observed.

***

"I'd have to say that while Hank and I were... let's say, finding Hollywood life a little heady, Josh Logan just didn't have a clue what

Hollywood was all about when he came out there," Stewart said. Making movies is a business, and he initially felt he could set Hollywood straight by demonstrating that commercial success was merely the icing on the cake. More important were integrity and art. And I believe we... That is, Hank and I... thought we knew more about creating movies than he did, even though none of us did at the time. Of course, the film industry is more complicated than that. You aim for what some may consider art, or at the very least good craftsmanship. But you also know that people have to see your work... a lot of people... because the films have to earn money for the company, or you'll be out of work soon. That's just business. Josh was a smart guy, but he hadn't realised it when he came to Hollywood.'

What Jim had realised was that the business of filmmaking demanded that only the few prestige films starring huge stars be lavished with time and money. 'The kind of film I was doing back then... they were mostly simply programmers.'

Stewart first learned to fly in 1936. He surprised himself by not learning to fly as rapidly as he should have: 'I just didn't do well at first... flying solo,' he said. After around eight hours, I should have been able to fly without an instructor, but it took me twice as long. I was too impatient and wanted to do things on my own... but the more impatient I became, the longer it took.Then, one day, while flying with my instructor, he asked me to perform a simulated forced landing. This required him to abruptly pull back on the throttle, as if the engine had failed. I quietly chose a field to land in... it was a potato field... and I was wonderfully gliding that baby in. The instructor was meant to give the plane power so that we could climb after checking that I was on target. But we just continued flying. I assumed the teacher had forgotten, gone out, or died, so I yanked on the throttle... but it wouldn't budge. We were almost on the ground by this point, so I didn't execute a simulated false landing--I did it for real. I felt I'd done well, but the instructor... he was irritated with me. He claimed he tried to gun the plane, but when the throttle wouldn't move, he assumed I was holding it on purpose. But I claimed that I had attempted to throttle the plane. That's when we realised the throttle was stuck.'He went on to say, "You realise that we actually had a real emergency." I thought to myself, "Just as well I didn't know that or I might not have done such a perfect emergency landing." After that, he assumed I'd be fine on my own.'

After obtaining his licence, Jim would get up before dawn every day, whether he was working or not, and drive down to the local airstrip, CloverField, for an hour of flying. Leland Hayward would frequently accompany him to the airstrip, but they always flew in separate planes.

Burgess Meredith wondered how much Hayward's willingness to drive to Clover Field with Jim had to do with whatever suspicions he had about his wife and Jim: 'I'm sure Hayward knew Jim held a candle for his wife, and I'd imagine he didn't want to take a chance that Jim might take Margaret up in his plane, so Hayward may have gone practically every day with Jim to the airfield... just to be sure. Despite this, Hayward never displayed signs of jealousy since Jim never gave him reason to be suspicious. Jim visited them frequently, and they were just three excellent friends. But I'll tell you something... Jim had feelings for her.'

Chapter 7: What Are We Going to Do With Jimmy Stewart?

Jim could afford to enjoy his social life with steady work and a regular salary. He was partying with Fonda, Joshua Logan, and Johnny Swope, who was working as an assistant director at the time. 'We were like the Four Musketeers,' Logan remarked. 'But, despite the fact that we were all great friends, Stewart and Fonda had a bond that was stronger than anything the four of us had ever had as a group.'

That closeness between Stewart and Fonda was viewed as more than just male friendship by Hollywood's vicious gossip mongers. 'We couldn't believe it when there were rumours that we were lovers, for God's sake!' Fonda recounted in 1976. Anyone who knew us knew we were only interested in women--and there were lots of them. I have no objections to homosexuality. Many men in the workplace have kept their homosexuality disguised for fear of jeopardising their careers. You've probably heard rumours about some of the men who were gay or bisexual. Some of those rumours have some validity to them. And, to be honest, I couldn't care less--or not much--if people want to accuse me because I believe I've had enough marriages to make me confident enough not to allow such charges to affect me. But Jim...! Those things hurt him a lot. He's a devout man who is so conservative that it offends my liberal soul. The very thought of Jim being a gay embarrasses him because it contradicts his principles in every way.He does not, however, pass judgement on homosexuals. He's a really non-judgmental type of guy since he recognizes that he's not the perfect man. He's not pretending to be. He used to play baseball as a young man, just like the rest of us. I'd even say he went above and above to debunk the rumors that we were a pair of gays. I never tried harder--I was always doing my best! Jim, on the other hand, went the additional mile!'

Some, including Joshua Logan, believed Jim had been 'playing the field' with 'considerable enthusiasm' since his arrival in Hollywood: 'It was my impression that Jim's womanising--which is what it was, however you try to tie it all up with a pretty ribbon--was due to the fact that he loved [Margaret] Sullavan and knew it would never lead to anything,' Logan said. 'So he saw almost every contract actress in town, as if he was just trying to get over her. Of course, he never did, but he gave it his all with Fonda's aid. People are aware of the sexual antics of housemates Errol Flynn and David Niven, but Fonda and Stewart were just as dynamic. They simply weren't the great stars that Flynn and Niven were at the time. And Flynn and Niven built a living by bragging about their sexual exploits. Fonda and Stewart never did, which is why people are constantly surprised when they hear about it.'

Fonda admitted in 1976 that he and Jim had "a whole lotta fun with the girls." The girls couldn't help but like Jim because he was always such a kind man. I had to keep an eye on things since a girl may be with me one minute and Jim the next. And he never seemed to encourage it in any way. "For Christ's sake, stop stealing my girls," I once said to him. "Gee, Hank, I'm sorry, but I don't steal them," he said. They steal me, you see." I could never get furious at him for that.'

Initially, all of Jim's female partners were contract players trying to achieve greater success like him. Norma Shearer, the Queen of the MGM lot, opted to be Jim's sweetheart during the first few months of 1937, kicking Jim's social life into high gear. Despite the fact that she had recently been widowed by the death of Metro's 'boy wonder' Irving Thalberg, she was 'spending little time mourning when there were so many young guys at the studio,' observed Joshua Logan. When Jimmy Stewart met her at Marion Davies' house for a costume party, he was six years her junior. Jimmy had been drinking a lot and emerging from his Pennsylvanian shell via an alcohol-induced haze.

When he spotted Shearer, he approached her and exclaimed, "You are the most beautiful creature I have ever seen." He had lighted up her yearning for him in that single drunken instant, and she regally took possession of him. It was too late by the time he regained consciousness. He was Norma Shearer's lover, and while the loving part tickled him, being chauffeured around town in her yellow limousine like a valued possession did not. You'd watch him sag in his seat, hoping that none of his pals would recognize him. She bought him a diamond-studded cigarette box so that whenever she asked him for a cigarette in front of others, the gift showed that he belonged to her.'

'I did see a lot of Norma Shearer... for a while,' Jim recounted. I doubt L B [Mayer] was overjoyed because she was such a great star and I was still a little player. He'd rather see her on Clark Gable's arm. Mayer never mentioned anything to me, but I heard there were... walls... certain grumblings.

'According to Josh Logan, I was a suppressed type of possession of hers. That's exactly what she wanted me to be. She gave me a diamond cigarette case and when I asked for a smoke, she'd respond, "Just a little thing I bought for Jim." That meant she'd purchased Jim. So, when she asked for a cigarette, I'd fumble around in all my pockets, asking, "Now where'd I put those cigarettes?" and eventually bring out a crumpled packet of Lucky Strikes.

"Now, I'm not saying I didn't have fun when I was with Norma... by golly, I did! But I didn't want to commit to a long-term relationship. I couldn't be blunt because I wasn't raised to be unfriendly to females... so I just continued giving her crumpled Lucky Strikes and did everything I could to hint that I wasn't her possession. I was also having fun with friends like Hank Fonda and Johnny Swope, and a lot of those nice moments were spent with... um... various girls. Finally, Norma got the message and gratefully let me go. I say "graciously" because she made it appear as if she was imparting some benevolent boon upon me by granting me my liberty.'

Jim had a less intense and more pleasurable affair with Ginger Rogers. According to Joshua Logan, Ginger's mother, Lela, arranged the marriage. 'Lela Rogers worked in the RKO publicity office, and RKO was where Ginger was making all those beautiful musicals with Fred Astaire,' Logan explained. RKO had a new actress, Lucille Ball, and Lela was doing everything she could to help her. At the same time, Ginger had divorced her husband, Lew Ayres, and Lela needed something-or someone-to distract Ginger from her worries. So Lela devised the plan of having Fonda and Stewart escort Ginger and Lucille around town, which would almost surely get Lucille some press. Jim liked to dance, so he was the logical option for Ginger's company, leaving Hank with Lucille.For a while, everything went swimmingly for all four. When they went dancing at the Trocadero and the Cocoanut Grove, Ginger believed Jim was a fantastic dancer, which he was. He could manoeuvre his long, lanky frame with ease. Hank simply lacked the same sense of rhythm.They went out to eat one night, and then the boys drove the girls back to their house. When the boys put the lights down low, Ginger and Lucille figured they were in for a night of exuberant love-making. 'All of a sudden, the lads rushed the girls into the kitchen to wash a week's worth of dirty dishes.'

'After dinner at a place called Barney's Beanery on Santa Monica Boulevard, we took the girls back to our apartment, and Jim and I were all set for a nice time, but Jim and Ginger chose to dance in and out of every room,' Fonda said. They were in the kitchen before I could say, "Jim, for God's sake, don't take her into the kitchen." And we had mounds of dishes that hadn't been washed in a week. That was a little much for Ginger. Lucille joined her as she began to wash the dishes. And we were extremely grateful. When they were finished, we expressed our appreciation.'

Fonda and Ball's pairing was not to last. 'Lucille constantly overdoes the make-up,' he observed. 'One night, she came out of the bathroom after God knows how long she had been in there putting on her paint, and when she came out, I couldn't help but think, "Yuk! Oh Christ!" And then Lucille went out, and that was the end of it. But Jim and Ginger--they were on a roll.'

When questioned by gossip journalist Sheilah Graham if she was in love with Stewart, Rogers said, 'If I'm not, I ought to be. He's the sweetest guy in Hollywood.'

Clarence Brown, one of MGM's finest filmmakers, had long desired to make Of Human Hearts. It was a rural life study based on Honoré Morrow's story 'Benefits Forgot,' with a somewhat dictatorial pastor and his rebellious son who aspires to escape his confined society to become a physician. The young guy travels to Baltimore to study medicine, assuming that his mother will cheerfully sell all of her belongings to support his education, even when his father dies and she is left alone and in need. When the Civil War breaks out, he is assigned to work in a field hospital on the front lines. He dismisses the numerous letters his mother sends him until Abraham Lincoln calls him to chastise him for his lack of gratitude to his mother. Finally, the young man sits down to compose a letter to his mother, and he is back on track.

Walter Huston was wonderful casting for the father, and Brown was persuaded James Stewart would be perfect as the grown-up son (Gene Reynolds played the younger version of the son). MGM executives were sceptical that Stewart had the depth required for the character, but Brown was persistent, and he got his way. Beulah Bondi played Jim's mother (for the second time).

The feedback was negative. Variety called the picture 'long on narrative and short on romance,' adding that the 'most cause for disappointment with the film is its plodding pace, and the defeatist attitude of the story.' The film was a flop, although Jim was praised for giving one of his best performances to date. 'I had a lot of fun making that picture,' he remarked. 'It was exactly what I needed. I thought I did quite well. The difficulty was that the studio was still unsure what to do with me. I could picture them pacing up and down in some executive office, wondering, "What shall we do with Jimmy Stewart?"

It's not surprising that Jim's next stop was RKO, where he co-starred with Ginger Rogers in Vivacious Lady. 'Oh, Ginger really liked Jim, and she wanted him to be in a picture with her,' Gloria explained. She got what she wanted since she was a big star at RKO.' Stewart portrayed a small-town botany professor who travels to New York to urge his playboy brother (James Ellison) to change his ways and ends up in a nightclub where he meets singer Ginger Rogers. They fall in love and marry, but when he brings her home, he lacks the confidence to declare her as his wife. He instead presents her as someone he met on a train. His life grows increasingly problematic until he musters the fortitude to confess the truth to both his parents and his now ex-fiancée (Frances Mercer). Beulah Bondi played his mother for the second time, while Charles Cobum played his father.

The film was basically an attempt to show that Rogers could carry a film without the help of Fred Astaire. However, by casting James Stewart as her co-star, she was only carrying half the film, with Jim proving to be a "priceless bit of casting," according to the New York Times at the time the film was released in 1938. The film was described as 'a good-natured, unsophisticated amusing comedy' by The New Yorker, and 'entertainment of the highest order and broadest appeal' by Variety. The general people agreed, and the picture was a great hit.

Making Vivacious Lady provided Jim and Ginger with a reason to pursue their amorous fling, but their romance was complicated when Jim's genuine love of the time, Margaret Sullavan, stepped in. Sullavan's new spouse, agent Leland Hayward (who was now also

Jim's agent), had gotten her a hefty deal with Metro-Goldwyn-Mayer. When Joan Crawford refused to play the lead in The Shopworn Angel, she stepped in. Producer Joseph L Mankiewicz had previously worked with Sullavan in Three Comrades and thought she would be a suitable replacement for Crawford. When Sullavan insisted on casting James Stewart beside her, Mankiewicz consented.

The Shopworn Angel was a remake of the 1928 part talkie, which was based on the play Private Pettigrew's Girl, which was inspired by a 1918 Saturday Evening Post tale. Sullavan portrayed a New York entertainer who is hit by a car and suffers minor injuries. The driver is a soldier (played by Stewart) set to deploy to war. In turn, he is smitten by her, pursues and woos her, and eventually marries her. She convinces herself that by marrying him, he will be safe in Europe's battlefields. He eventually goes off to war, and she learns of his death while performing in a bar one night.

When it was released in 1938, reviews were divided over the picture and Stewart's performance. According to Variety, "it is only occasionally] credible screen drama." Margaret Sullavan delivers a strong performance that is rich in depth and eloquence. 'James Stewart is a natural enough rookie, but his performance lacks character.'

The film, according to the New York Herald, "boasts of two of the finest actors appearing on the screen today... [Sullavan] has invested scene after scene with eloquence and vigour." Her voice has a certain sound to it, and her every movement exudes authority. Similarly, James Stewart brings the Texas private to life and keeps the character solid and compelling even when the writing provides him little help.'

'Jim had two enormous plusses going for him in that [picture],' Gloria, who was never jealous of Jim's connection with Sullavan, remarked. And both were genuine. The first was his bad driving, and the second was his crush on Margaret.

'Everyone expected Jim and Sullavan to have chemistry when they first appeared on the screen. According to Jim, she offered him more direction than the director [H C Potter], and he learned something new about film acting every time he worked with her. But what truly worked for him was that they built chemistry together--much like Tracy and Hepburn, only Tracy and Hepburn had a lifelong love affair.'

Gloria believed that Stewart and Sullavan's love was consummated, but only in the beginning. 'Of course he adored her,' she explained. 'Every man fell in love with her. And she was well aware of it. She made use of men. But she never made use of Jim. That is why I believe she adored him. Of course, they had an affair when they fell in love. But when Jim saw Fonda would be hurt, and Sullavan kept marrying, he gave her up. Jim is not a moron. He knew his connection with Fonda was eternal, and if he married Sullavan, his friendship with Hank would be over. And he knew that if he and Sullavan got together, let alone married, it would result in acrimony, thereby ending his friendship with both Fonda and Sullavan. So he admired her from afar and maintained friendships with his two best friends... before he met me. I then became his best friend.'

One of Jim's other close buddies was film director Frank Capra--or would be soon. He was one of Columbia's most influential directors, producing hits like It Happened One Night, Lost Horizon, and Mr. Deeds Goes to Town. Capra had watched several of Jim's films and thought he would be ideal for a major role in You Can't Take It With You, based on George S Kaufman and Moss Hart's Pulitzer Prize-winning play. Capra's insistence that he borrow Stewart from MGM was granted by Columbia boss Harry Cohn; Capra always got his way at Columbia because everything he produced there throughout the 1930s resulted in large box office takings and thirteen Oscars in total.

The picture was a wild comedy with a somewhat serious philosophical theme, as was typical of Capra's work. It all revolves around the Vanderhoff family, which is ruled over by Lionel Barrymore as a former businessman who feels that the best things in life are unrelated to what his money can purchase. A daughter who wants to be a playwright and artist; a son-in-law who wants to design the ideal firecracker; a granddaughter who wants to be a ballerina; and her husband who plays the xylophone round out the dysfunctional family. Another granddaughter, Jean Arthur, is a secretary who falls in love with her boss, Jimmy Stewart.

There are also a slew of other strange personalities who aren't linked yet have odd motives to be in and out of the house. The relationship between Stewart and Jean Arthur, however, is the film's heart and the basis for much of its comedy.

Jim remembered Capra and Arthur fondly. 'Capra was not only a wonderful filmmaker, but also a nice guy,' he remarked. We clicked right instantly and have remained friends ever since.' Capra would later seek Stewart's assistance when he was accused of being a Communist during the McCarthy era Hollywood witch-hunts.

'Jean was an insecure kind of girl,' Jim remarked of Arthur. She was a fantastic performer... but she didn't seem to realise it.' When Capra recalled, 'Jean was always outstanding, top class-when she was on the set,' he was a little less kind, but honest. The issue was getting her to the set. She refused to leave the changing room. She was convinced that she would never be any good out there. Despite this, she was consistently good, day after day, scene after scene. I've never seen her perform poorly.'

'I knew Jean a bit,' Gloria recounted. Some people were nasty to her because she was so insecure. But she had anxiety--almost a phobia--about acting. She was worried that one bad performance would ruin everything and end her career. Jim didn't think her anxiety was something to be condemned. He just recognized her brilliance and did everything he could to support her. In the movies, he was still a little green, but he provided her support and understanding. I don't think she ever got over her anxiety, but when they worked together, he was very patient with her because he knew she'd be great once the cameras were rolling. But it did wear him out. There were days when he returned home from the studio and remarked, "I love Jean, and God knows I feel sorry for her problem, but dealing with it sure wears you down." "Let Capra deal with it," I said. "But she's my screen partner," he explained. I want her to feel at ease with me. She needs to know I care." I still thought he should have left Capra worried about everything, but that's Jim--he's just a nice man from Indiana.'

Capra had only kind things to say about Stewart, stating in 1980, 'On the one hand, he was a typical guy. He liked to hang around and converse with the cast members, but he never sought intimate friendships. It just occurred that someone became his friend. He didn't look for buddies. But he was pleasant to everyone. And then he'd wander off on his own because he just needed some peaceful time to himself. I'm not sure what he was thinking about. 'I thought that asking would be an imposition.'Stewart has a strange obsession with comic books. He'd sit there and read comic books. I believe Flash Gordon was his favourite. It was so typical of Jim, I thought. He may be serious about his work and get lost in contemplation, yet he can also be the youngster he was in Indiana reading comic books.He's a nice guy who is also very professional and accomplished. People still believe they know James Stewart because they recall films like It's a Wonderful Life and say, "Yeah, that's what he's always like." I'm not sure why that is with Jim. You can say that about someone like John Wayne or Clark Gable and know it's mostly accurate. However, Jimmy Stewart portrayed a wide range of personalities. He wasn't always the same persona, and I get irritated when people assume he was. True, he has a completely

Jimmy Stewart charisma--and I suppose that's what people really mean when they say he's always the same--but he's a highly skilled actor with many layers.

'One of the best things about Jimmy Stewart for me as a director is that I don't have to argue with him or waste time trying to explain his purpose. "Look, Jim, it's like this..." I say, and he says, "I got it," and then he does it. I wish every actor was like that. So, after You Can't Take It With You, I was always looking for another opportunity to collaborate with him.'

You Can't Take It With You, which was released in 1938, was a tremendous hit with both viewers and critics. It also received Oscar nods for Best Picture and Best Director, as well as screenplay by Robert Riskin, cinematography by Joseph Walker, and Best Supporting Actress for Spring Byington's performance as the daughter.

Stewart's films from 1938 to 1939 kept him busy, and he was in such high demand from other studios that he was frequently loaned elsewhere. Stewart was filming away from his home studio immediately after finishing You Can't Take It With You. This time it was for David Selzniek at United Artists, who co-starred him in the tearjerker Made For Each Other with Carole Lombard.

Stewart played a calm lawyer who humbly served his demanding boss (Charles Cobum) and whose marriage (to Lombard) was continually on the rocks. When the couple's little boy becomes unwell and serum must be flown in at significant expense, Stewart musters the fortitude to confront his supervisor and demand the money he requires. As the pilot transporting the serum confronts a violent storm that threatens to wreck his plane, Stewart and Lombard find themselves in a race against time.

The picture marked a change for Lombard from her customary

wisecracking comedy. Jim remembered her notorious usage of four-letter expletives from the stage. 'Carole Lombard could curse like no other woman I ever knew,' he remarked. Other ladies swear... but Carole did it with grace. I don't like hearing women swear... It's kind of awkward. But Lombard... she was the only girl I'd seen who could let off a stream of four-letter obscenities and not humiliate you... because she did it in a ladylike manner.'

He returned to MGM for The Ice Follies of 1939 (filmed in 1938 for a 1939 release). The picture, touted as a musical extravaganza on ice, starred Joan Crawford as a singing ice-skating sensation who earns a film deal, while her skater-choreographer husband, played by Stewart, tries to stage a major ice show. Their jobs keep them apart until Crawford decides to prioritise her marriage over her career. Happily, in the grand tradition of Hollywood, Stewart's ice show is made into a film, with Crawford as the star. The film failed partly because Crawford couldn't sing--four of her six songs were cut--and neither Crawford nor Stewart could ice dance convincingly. MGM seemed to be wondering, 'What shall we do with Jimmy Stewart?'

Following that, he starred in the screwball comedy It's a Wonderful World as a rookie private eye convicted of a murder he didn't commit and escaping from prison. He sets out to solve the crime with the help of a crazy poetess played by Claudette Colbert. Woody 'One Take' Van Dyke, who directed Jim in Rose Marie and After the Thin Man, directed it in just twelve days.

Stewart has worked with such prominent females as Jean Harlow, Joan Crawford, Margaret Sullavan, Ginger Rogers, Jean Arthur, Eleanor Powell, and Claudette Colbert in just four years. His popularity with audiences had grown, and by 1939, he had ascended to become a popular star at the Metro-Goldwyn-Mayer studio, although not being in the same category as Clark Gable or Robert Taylor. However, he was constantly second-billed to the leading lady, and his own studio was unsure what to do with him to make him a top-tier movie star.

It was up to filmmaker Frank Capra of Columbia Studios to cast him in the part that would propel him to stardom. Mr. Smith Goes to Washington was the title of the film.

Chapter 8: Star Status

'At the time, what I really wanted to do was produce a film about Chopin,' Frank Capra told me in 1980. So I went to visit Harry Cohn and informed him, and he said, "Forget it." Please give me another Mr. Deeds."

'I went on to say, "I've already made Mr. Deeds."

'So I rushed out of the office, swearing I'd never make another picture in my life, and was preparing to leave when a writer named Sam Briskin came in and said, "I'd heard you had a row with Harry Cohn." He held up a two-page blueprint and said, "Take a look at this."

'The film was titled The Man From Montana. I blurted out, "This sounds like a goddamn Western." He explained, "Just read it." "Forget it," I responded. "I'm going."

'I then read it. It was about an honest young senator who exposes senate corruption and tries to prevent a measure from passing by delivering a 24-hour speech--what we term a "filibuster." I urged my secretary to stop packing my belongings, walked to Sam, and told him, "You're so goddamn right. This is a better narrative than Mr. Deeds Goes to Town. We'll call it Mr. Smith Goes to Washington, and Gary Cooper will play the lead.' When I returned to Cohn with this, he was so relieved that I'd forgotten about making Chopin's life a living hell that he gave the green light on Mr. Smith right away. I was all set to cast Copper in the role when I began to consider Jimmy Stewart. There were many cinematic roles that fit Cooper and Stewart; they were both kind of folksy in their own ways. Both were ideal for the role of Mr. Smith. However, because Stewart was younger, he was a better fit for the role than Cooper. He still had the appearance of a farm child. He had strong principles of his own, and they would manifest themselves on the screen. Mr. Smith reminded me of James Stewart in many respects. 'I also believed that, given the filibuster situation, Stewart was better qualified as an actor technically.'

Capra and his screenwriter, Sidney Buchman, travelled to Washington in October 1938 to begin work on Mr. Smith Goes to Washington. Capra was surprised to receive an invitation to visit the FBI from J Edgar Hoover while he was there. Capra was escorted to the FBI handgun range, where he practised firing a Thompson submachine gun, among other things. Hoover personally emailed Capra a photograph of this occasion. Capra had no idea Hoover was practically spying on him--something he would discover in due course and seek assistance from Jimmy Stewart.

Jim described Frank Capra as "his favourite director." (He also used to consider Anthony Mann to be one of his two favourite directors, but the schism that occurred in 1957 put an end to that.) 'Capra always did a lot of coverage on any incident,' Jim said. He'd perform take after take, from nearly every possible angle. He was continuously striving to capture the best possible image on film.He offered me a ride home in his car one day and asked if I wanted to look at the day's rushes on the way. At his home, he had his own screening room. Wall, I never went to watch any rushes because I despised seeing this young, gangly kid on the screen, and I was always convinced that one day the audience would feel the same way... so I reasoned that if I avoided seeing me, no one else would see what I always saw. But, not wanting to anger Capra, I consented. Wall, I was there for nearly two hours seeing rushes. Every single photo from that day was there-take after take, from every viewpoint.'I couldn't say no when he invited me to come see the rushes the next day. I'd been watching the rushes for three hours and they hadn't finished yet. Then I discovered Capra had dozed out. I couldn't leave without telling him, yet I couldn't wake him up. So I had to sit through the rushes, which were excruciating for me. When he finally awoke, I told him, "Frank, I have to be honest with you. I despise watching these shows. I appreciate you inviting me to see them with you, but I don't want to see them any longer." I expected him to be angry and give me a hard time about it, but instead he remarked, "Why didn't you say something earlier?" Of course, you are not required to watch the rushes." As a result, I never watched them again.'

Capra had recruited Jean Arthur to play Jim, but Capra claimed that Jim was so preoccupied with his profession that he didn't have as much time to spend to the actress as she would have liked. He was trying his hardest to get everything just right, and Jean felt he should have paid more attention to her neuroses. She spent a lot of time vomiting up in her dressing room because she was more insecure than ever. Perhaps she simply wants Jimmy's attention. She never spoke kindly of him again for a long time after that.' Jean Arthur's career was cut short by Mr. Smith. She did seven additional films until 1944, when Columbia let her go, after which she only made A Foreign Affair in 1948 and Shane in 1953.

Jim faced some of the most difficult tasks while playing Mr. Smith:

'The most difficult thing for me was finding the correct tone in my voice for the filibuster. Mr. Smith speaks for twenty-four hours before getting a sore throat and his voice becoming scratchy. When Capra heard my practised gruff rasp, he remarked, "Jim, that's just awful." You're meant to have a sore throat, but you sound like an actor attempting to sound raspy." I responded by saying, "That's exactly the position I find myself in." "Well, keep trying," he said. You've got to do a better job with that situation."

'This made me quite concerned. So I went to an ear, nose, and throat specialist and asked him if there was anything that could cause me to have a sore throat. He seemed shocked, because people normally ask him to assist them get rid of a sore throat, and here I was asking him to give me one. He went on to say, "Do you realise it's taken me twenty-five years of hard study and practice to cure sore throats?" "Doc, I really need a sore throat," I remarked. I'm in a movie, and I need to have a sore throat and sound like I have a sore throat." "All Hollywood people are crazy," he added, "but you take the cake." Okay, I'll give you the worst throat pain you've ever had, but don't whine when it hurts like hell." I told him that I wouldn't, so he injected some dichloride of mercury into my throat--just a drop--and he had to put it near my vocal cords without touching them. "How's that?" he asked. I couldn't speak, and when I asked, "How does it sound?" it sounded like a really horrible rasp--a true rasp. And he replied, "You got it, all right."

'In the end, the doctor was glad of my business since I hired him to come on set and watch me while my throat was hurting. So you'll know I've got a sore throat when you see the filibuster scene.'

Mr. Smith Goes to Washington was released in 1939 to excellent reviews and earned Jim his highest personal notices to date. 'With the exception of a few flights into the extracallow, James Stewart offers the most convincing portrayal of his career as a home-made warrior against political corruption,' commented Newsweek. 'Now he is mature and provides a challenging part, with numerous nuances, moments of tragicomic impact,' said The Nation of Stewart. And he can do more than just play solitary scenes well. He demonstrates his character's strength via experience. Finally, he is so powerful that his victory is completely credible.' Stewart's Mr. Smith was described by the New York Times as "a joy for this season, if not forever."

Jim received the New York Film Critics Award for his efforts in providing his best performance to date. He was nominated for an Oscar for Goodbye, Mr. Chips, but lost to Robert Donat.

The film's positive reviews may have spared it from being cancelled amid a storm of political outrage. 'I never really thought about it when we were making it, but it was a delicate subject,' Jim said. It was shown in Washington, and the entire Senate and Congress were present... and half of them walked out. Even back then, they were troubled by the prospect of high-level corruption.'

Capra was charged by Democrat James Byrnes of compromising everything precious to America. The US ambassador to the United Kingdom, Joseph Kennedy, told Harry Cohn and Columbia that the picture would be perceived as Nazi propaganda by Europeans. The large studios put roughly $2 million in a bucket to bribe Columbia to shelve the picture because they were afraid of a severe retaliation from the Senate. But Cohn stayed fast and refused to have the film banned. Despite the political uproar, it was well on its way to becoming a hit, thanks to favourable reviews and an enthusiastic reception from preview audiences. Mr. Smith Goes to Washington may not have been popular with politicians, but it was a big success with the rest of America. As a result, James Stewart became a prominent influence in Hollywood. He was now a celebrity.

Jim had performed almost every type of role available at MGM--except a cowboy. Universal came up with the bold notion after acquiring him on loan for their Western Destry Rides Again. George Marshall, a veteran of many cowboy sagas, directed the film.

When Destry Rides Again was released in 1939, most Westerns were B-movies aimed at unsophisticated viewers who wanted action but didn't care about quality. However, just a few Westerns were released that year, including two from John Ford-Stagecoach and Drums Along the Mohawk-Michael Curtiz's Dodge City, Henry King's Jesse James, and Cecil B DeMille's Union Pacific.

Destry Rides Again was a sensual spoof, tailor-made for seductive Marlene Dietrich, which set it apart from other B-Westerns. Her career was truly in a slump, and she needed an image to help boost her fame. Joe Pasternak, the producer, came up with the idea of starring Dietrich in a sensual Western frolic; her salary was only $75,000, a sixth of what she was paid at her home studio, Paramount.

'Joe Pasternak had a... er... vision about Dietrich singing "The Boys in the Backroom"... and he wanted to make it come true,' Jim remembered of Pasternak's decision to cast Dietrich in "Destry Rides Again". He imagined her as a bar-room girl in black stockings singing a "Lili Marlene" song. And he didn't only want her for the film... he wanted her... something she was well aware of. He didn't win her over.'

What Jim didn't say was that the man who got Dietrich was himself. 'Oh, Dietrich wanted Jim as soon as she saw him,' Burgess Meredith recalled. And men couldn't get enough of Marlene. She was not your ordinary love-maker, to put it mildly. She was skilled in a variety of stunts. So once she had seduced a man, he was hers till she grew tired of him.She was skilled at exploiting a man's flaw. Jim was in his dressing room one day when she shut him in and told him she was returning with a surprise. She had discovered that Jim enjoyed reading comic books and was a fan of Flash Gordon. Marlene had gone to the props department and requested that a life-size doll of Flash Gordon be made. Then she locked him in his dressing room and had the boys bring over the Flash Gordon doll, so when she opened the door for him, he saw this life-size Flash Gordon she'd constructed for him--and he was hers.'

Away from the set, Jim and Dietrich spent evenings eating and making love at night, with Dietrich teaching him things he'd never dreamed of,' according to Meredith. Jim never officially admitted to having an affair with Dietrich, but he did tell me in 1981, "That was such a long time ago-in another lifetime." But, yeah, we had a good time together... nothing serious... just horsing around.' Gloria stated that she was aware Jim and Dietrich were a "hot item."

Dietrich, on the other hand, never mentioned their romance in her memoir Marlene Dietrich: My Life, although rumours circulated that Dietrich had fallen pregnant by him and that he insisted on having the child terminated. Burgess Meredith stated, "If you ask me, Dietrich started those rumours." When Jim told her it was over, I believe she believed it was an unforgivable sin.'

Gloria had no idea Jim had forced Dietrich to undergo an abortion. 'No one forces Dietrich to do anything she doesn't want to do. And Jim despises the mere idea of abortion. It's just not a part of his belief system.'

Meredith believed he knew why Stewart had parted ways with Dietrich. 'She was bisexual, and she liked both men and women. I believe Jim appreciated Dietrich's somewhat extreme sexual abilities--at least, by his standards--but when she tried to persuade him to have a girlfriend of hers join them, he drew the line. And he finished it, which she couldn't forgive. So I suppose she spread that rumour, but no one believed it. For Christ's sake, we're talking about Jimmy Stewart. Furthermore, Jim was unaware that, while she was seeing him, she was also seeing Erich Maria Remarque [the author of All Quiet on the Western Front]. I know she was The Blue Angel and all, but she wasn't an angel.'

'I thought by then I understood pretty much all there was to know about acting for cinema... but then she catches me doing something,' Jim said of Dietrich's professional relationship with him on the set. "When the camera is shooting over my shoulder and on you, you tend to look at me in one eye and then the other," she explained. The camera detects this and intensifies it, causing your eyes to flick from left to right and back again." "But that's what happens in real life," I pointed out. You can't gaze at something with both eyes open. You shift your attention from one eye to the other." "Yes, but it's distracting when caught on camera," she explained. Look into just one eye--it doesn't matter if it's the left or right eye--just one eye."

And she was correct, and I've been doing it ever since.'

'Pasternak didn't want me for the picture,' Jim knew. He desired Gary Cooper. I believe I was less expensive than Coop... therefore... I got the part. Coop was supposed to play a man riding into town to avenge his father's death. Pasternak didn't think I could play a role like that when he cast me, so he made my character a deputy in this wide-open village who doesn't believe in carrying a pistol. But eventually, he needs to draw his gun... and that, I always felt, cleared the door for Shane. And that concept piqued my interest. This, I believed, made for a distinct kind of Western.'Because of the famous saloon brawl between Dietrich and Una Merkel, the public had a difficult time remembering me in the picture. I recall shooting the scenario. Those girls truly gave each other hell... and they seemed to enjoy it. They were fighting and kicking each other, and I was afraid that someone might get wounded. But they were having so much fun that it was entertaining to watch. The brawl ends when I have to pour a pail of water over them. You'd be shocked how much water is contained in a bucket. George Marshall, the director, had me hurl bucket after bucket over them, in long shot and close-up. I had so much fun dumping buckets of water on those two girls. When Life magazine published a feature on the film, they wanted a shot of me pouring water on Dietrich and Merkel for the cover, so I gotta do it all over again. The critics didn't realise it at the time, but the film was a satire on the type of Western Tom Mix used to create.'

When "Destry Rides Again" was published in 1940, Bosley Crowther of the New York Times praised Stewart's portrayal as "a masterpiece of underplaying in a deliberately sardonic vein-the freshest, most offbeat characterisation that this popular actor ever played." It was much better, in my opinion, than the rambunctious young senator [in Mr. Smith Goes to Washington].' According to Time magazine, Stewart "turns in a performance as good as or better [than Mr. Smith]."

Despite the accolades and success, Jim's own studio executives looked perplexed that he had been cast in a Western; it had never occurred to them that he might be a cowboy-type. 'They [MGM] felt justified in believing I couldn't play a cowboy because once Destry was out, I got emails from Western aficionados stating I did everything wrong as a Western sheriff,' Jim explained. They claimed I lacked toughness. But no one was making Westerns for... intelligent audiences at the time. They were all B-movies about good guys hunting bad guys, and they all looked the same, featured the same performers, and used the same sets. Destry Rides Again reached a far larger audience.'

That expanded audience helped James Stewart become one of MGM's biggest stars. Fans of cowboy films, on the other hand, would take a little longer to accept James Stewart as a big Western actor alongside John Wayne and Gary Cooper.

MGM, on the other hand, saw fit to pair him with Margaret Sullavan in The Shop Around the Corner. Ernst Lubitsch, who produced and directed the film, came up with the idea to couple them. The scenario takes place in a gift shop, where Stewart's character, the chief cashier, keeps everything going smoothly. In search of romance, he meets Margaret Sullavan, who plays a female letter buddy. Due to the Christmas rush, the shop advertises for a new salesperson, and Sullavan applies. When Stewart interviews her, he rejects her application, but the shop's manager (played by Frank Morgan) overturns his decision and hires her. Stewart and Sullavan despise each other despite the fact that they are lovers through correspondence. Much of the comedy in the film consequently revolves around the pen pals' attempts to meet up, only to find themselves face to face and squabbling. The film cleverly used Stewart and Sullavan's connection as two people who appear to despise each other yet discover they are in love.

'Margaret had recently had a kid, and Jim was dating a number of other women,' Gloria explained. Lubitsch realised that by casting Jim and Margaret, they would have the chemistry that had always existed between them on the screen, but their private lives would offer the distance that the plot demanded. And he was correct. Margaret was always quite skilled at saying and doing things to irritate people, and she could even irritate Jim.' 'I could never be upset with Margaret for long, even though she said and did a lot of things that riled a lot of other people,' Stewart added. We had a scene in a restaurant, and one of my lines was, "I will go out on the street and roll my trousers up to my knees." Wall, I just couldn't say the line correctly, and she was furious. I was standing there with my pants rolled up to my knees, which I despised since I had skinny legs and felt weird, so I couldn't recite the phrase correctly. "This is just ridiculous," Margaret exclaimed. For God's sake, say the line." "I don't want to do this scene today," I retorted. They should have cast someone else with good legs in the role. I really don't feel like doing this scene today."

'"Are you refusing to work?" she said."Yes," I responded, and she replied, "Then I refuse to take the picture." That halted me in my tracks... I could feel her rage directed directly at me. "I changed my mind," I explained. Let's get started." So we finished it.

'You never knew what she'd do when the cameras were rolling, which made the task so interesting. She didn't do anything really noteworthy. It was always the minor details. You'd do a scene and she'd utter a few words differently than usual, or she'd do something with her eyes, like give you a look she never gave you in rehearsal. And, while they were minor details, they were significant to her because they made all the difference in a scene, and a camera would catch up on those nuances, which was part of what made her so good.She also despised much talk. "We're talking too much, and we don't need all these words to show the audience what we mean," she'd say some days. We can do it with just a glance." It was critical for her to get the correct expression from me. When the camera was only on me, she loved to do tiny things like stick her tongue out at me as I was trying to remember my lines and get the mood correct... and I'd get extremely irritated... which was precisely the right reaction. She made all the difference, like getting me to grin in a particular way. Now I can smile with the best of them, but she'd just stare at me all soft and gooey... and I'd deliver the perfect smile. And if I gave her the wrong look, even if she wasn't in the picture, she'd yell, "Stop right there. What in the world are you doing? "You're not making me feel the way I should." And that's what I'd say: "You're not even in the shot so how's anybody gonna know?" And she'd say, "I'll let you know." And then I'd just burst out laughing.'

The picture received positive reviews upon its initial release in 1940. Variety praised the picture for generating 'humour and human interest from what appear to be insignificant situations,' adding that 'it proceeds further to impress with the great characteristics by Margaret Sullavan and James Stewart.' The film won over critics over the years, and the New Yorker dubbed it "one of the most beautifully acted and paced romantic comedies ever made in this country" in 1978.

Stewart and Sullavan teamed up again in The Mortal Storm, which was shot in 1939 and published in 1940. With the Second World War raging in Europe and America remaining neutral, Hollywood studios produced a number of films aimed at demonstrating sympathy for the suffering Allied soldiers and scorn for the Nazi party. MGM, on the other hand, attempted to obscure its condemnation of the Nazis by locating The Mortal Storm Somewhere in Europe,' despite the fact that the movie is plainly set in Germany. The plot revolved around a family led by a biology professor (Frank Morgan). The family is divided into two factions: those who support Hitler and those who do not. Stewart becomes an outlaw when, as a suitor to the professor's daughter (Margaret Sullavan), he assists a Jewish professor in escaping over the Alps. Stewart tries to lead Sullavan to safety after she becomes a Nazi enemy, but she is shot and murdered.

'It was blatantly anti-Nazi, and the filmmaker [Frank Borzage] only made a meager effort to cover the truth,' Stewart remarked of the picture. In fact, it was so evident that a German delegate warned Metro that after Germany won the war, they would not forget our photograph. Actually, it appeared at the moment that they would win the war since France was going to fall. But Borzage, Margaret, myself, and a few others declared that we didn't care about the threats. But Robert Young was concerned. He had a wife and children to consider. Fortunately, nothing bad happened to Bob or his family, and it's possible that I and some of the others who didn't take the threat seriously were simply too naive to realise that if Germany had won the war, we'd be in tremendous danger... just for making a movie. In the end, I believe that was an indication of the war's fight for liberty.'

MGM capitalised on Stewart and Sullavan's casting, proclaiming The Mortal Storm to be "the love story of today with the popular sweethearts from The Shop Around the Corner." However, the chemistry that The Shop Around the Corner had relied on was overshadowed by the darker components of this film's tale, and both critics and the general public were less enthused about this film than they had been about the former. The New York Herald Tribune called it "dated and romantically distorted," but praised Stewart for "acting with such intense sincerity that the personal tragedy at the heart of the piece is the most satisfying note in the proceedings."

'I guess not all the critics loved the picture... notably Josef Goebbels, who despised what we had to say about the Nazis and prohibited all MGM films from showing in Germany,' Jim recalled. And because we irritated Mr. Goebbels, I guess the picture was a success.'

Chapter 9: A Commission and an Oscar

Most Americans did not believe that the war occurring in Europe had anything to do with them in 1939. Jim had a different perspective. His first active role in the war was to invest in what would become a flying school founded by Leland Hayward, Jack Connelly (a Civil Aeronautics Authority engineering inspector), and Johnny Swope. It was in response to an effort by US Army General 'Hap' Arnold to prepare the US Air Force for war. He pushed civilian aviators to establish flying schools that could be used as Air Force training facilities if war broke out.

Hayward, Connelly, and Swope persuaded Jim, as well as Henry Fonda and Cary Grant, to participate in their Southwest Airways firm. They bought Sky Harbour Air Service in Phoenix, Arizona, and renamed it Thunderbird Field.

'I just thought that the war would surely involve America,' Jim explained, 'and that it was vital to create areas where the Air Force could train its pilots, because there simply weren't the facilities to teach them. At the time, our air force was inferior to that of many other countries. So I made an investment that took a long time to pay off, but that wasn't the plan in the first place. The profit came from what the institution accomplished, which was to train thousands of pilots. Thunderbird Field II and Falcon Field were added as new facilities. Pilots from the Allies came to train in those locations. It was a worthwhile endeavour, and I was honoured to be a part of it.'

Before the end of 1939, Stewart was moved by MGM to Warner Brothers in return for Olivia de Havilland. MGM required de Havilland for David Selznick's Gone With the Wind, and Warners, who was under contract with Miss de Havilland, accepted Stewart as a fair trade, putting him in the romantic comedy No Time For Comedy, based on S N Behrman's hit Broadway play.

Jim portrayed a wealthy playwright who writes a string of comedies for his actress wife, Rosalind Russell. But he notices that his aptitude for comedy is fading. He becomes entangled with a flirtatious socialite (Genevieve Tobin), and concludes that he must create a socially significant drama. His marriage survives a series of love snafus, as does his ability for creating blockbuster comedy.

When it was released in 1940, the film was well-received by the general audience, but many critics couldn't help but use the title to express their thoughts about it. However, the film was successful enough that it was reissued several years later under the title Guy With a Grin.

Olivia de Havilland and James Stewart became a romantic couple after being swapped by their respective studios. 'For Jim, Olivia looked like the genuine thing,' Burgess Meredith, who was now sharing the Brentwood bachelor pad, recalled. I'm convinced they were in love, even if they pretended to be just playing the game. Olivia performed admirably in the game. Whenever a reporter asked if she planned to marry Jim, she responded yes, but in such a way that it sounded frivolous. Jim never denied the charges, and I know he once asked her to marry him, but he didn't seem real about it, and they both laughed at the idea. But I'm convinced there was a burgeoning affection hidden underneath the fun.'I believe she was more excited about him than he was about her. I believe he was frightened of falling in love with an actress because he knew such a relationship, if it progressed to marriage, would fail. As a result, he maintained an emotional distance. He was the same with all of his women, I'd say. He enjoyed entertaining them, but they were never the most important things in his life. His work was more vital. That, I believe, was his safety net. Things would never grow too serious if he didn't offer them his undivided attention and attention.But it was Margaret Sullavan who kept Jim from committing his entire heart to one lady at the moment. He'd never confess it, but he still loved her despite knowing he'd never have her.'

James Stewart had one of his biggest triumphs with Destry Rides Again, which was solely filmed to prevent Marlene Dietrich's career collapse. Because of the waning career of another great actress, Katharine Hepburn, he was going to achieve even more success in 1940.

Hepburn was a savvy businesswoman who wanted to break out of her rut by purchasing the rights to the hugely successful play The Philadelphia Story and then selling them to the highest bidder. This was revealed to be MGM.

The plot revolved around Tracy Lord and George Kittredge's society wedding. C K Dexter Haven, Tracy's ex-husband, still loves her, but when he learns that a magazine is planning to print a scandalous article about Tracy's estranged father, he bravely intervenes and strikes a deal with the editor, arranging for a reporter and a photographer to cover the high-society wedding. Tracy remarries Dexter after her emotions become jumbled and things become complicated.

By having casting approval, Hepburn maintained control over the production, and the first piece of casting was herself, as Tracy Lord. She had hoped for Spencer Tracy and Clark Gable to play the reporter and ex-husband, but she was content with James Stewart and Cary Grant.

'When I read the script, I assumed I'd be offered the part of the fella who's going to marry Katharine Hepburn,' Jim recounted. "The reporter is a much more interesting role," I kept thinking. If only I could play that part." But I was fine with playing the bad guy until I was told, "But you are playing the reporter." That was the nicest part for me. It was even greater than Cary Grant's role.' Grant was aware that his position was little, but he accepted it since he had been given top billing as well as the highest salary, $137,500. His entire remuneration was donated to the British War Relief Fund.

Jim debunked the long-held belief that the film's director, George Cukor, was primarily a "director for actresses": "Cukor could direct any actor." He told you what he wanted, but he also let you be free. Cary Grant and I had a small bit where we're talking, and we got off the script somehow, but we carried right on... just ad-libbing but maintaining in character... and Cukor stayed right on recording, and he was so delighted with the results that he put that take in the finished film.' He said about Audrey Hepburn:

'I had a great time working with Katharine. She was entertaining... but she was serious about the film. When I had to do a part in a swimming suit... waall, I just told Katharine that I looked awful in a bathing suit since my legs were just so... skinny. "Show me your legs," she commanded authoritatively, and I lifted my jeans up till she could see my knees... and she took one glance and replied, "You're correct. Those are the ugliest legs I've ever seen." So she persuaded Cukor to let me do the sequence in my bathrobe.'She was quite capable in issuing orders. One night... it was a Friday... as we were wrapping up for the day, she remarked, "I'd like to come flying with you tomorrow." I'll meet you at Clover Field at 8:00 a.m." So I arrived in the morning... and she was already there. And she was asking about everything from the moment I started the engine... so I tried to answer all of her questions. I'd started the engine when she yelled, "Wait! "Is the oil gauge below the red line?" So I informed her, "That's always the way it works." And she said, "But the oil shouldn't be below the red marker." "But Kate," I responded, "it always works this way." And she kept talking about it, so I just let the engine run for a little while longer. "The oil is still not on red," she said as we drove by. I told her, "Don't worry about it." "Make sure you achieve the correct speed before you lift off," she added, and I replied, "Don't worry, Kate. I'd like to make it through this takeoff as well." As we ascended higher, she just kept yelling instructions at me.

'I decided to drive her up to Saugus, but just as I was about to turn, she yelled, "Don't turn!" So I ascended to 500 feet, then 800 feet, and finally 1,000 feet, where I was about to turn when she yelled, "No, don't turn!" When I tried to turn again, she said, "Don't turn!" I muttered to myself, "Kate, if we don't turn we'll be in China!" "All right," she answered, "you can turn."

'"I thought we'd go up to Saugus," I said, and she replied, "The oil gauge is still below the red." "I'd like to return." So I circled Clover Field as we lost altitude... and all the time she was directing me what to do and what not to do... and I knew she wasn't moving her gaze away from the oil gauge. When we landed... well, it wasn't really a landing--it was more like a controlled crash--she said, "Thank you," curtly, hopped out of the plane, went straight to her car, and drove away... and she never mentioned flying to me again. '

Congress approved legislation in September 1940 authorising the annual drafting of 900,000 men between the ages of twenty and thirty-six. Two of MGM's top performers, James Stewart and Robert Montgomery, announced their intentions to Louis B Mayer right away.

'Mayer just couldn't get it,' Jim explained. '"You don't have to enlist," he said. Wait till they draft you, and then we'll exclude you both." He promised me that there would be a slew of photos that were better than any I'd seen before. He promised me almost anything in order to persuade me to change my viewpoint. I informed him that I had no intention of requesting for exemption and would instead volunteer. By that point, any rational person could see that America would be drawn into the conflict. It was a worldwide struggle. 'How could we not participate?'

'Jim comes from a family who never shirked their responsibilities when their country was at war, and he wasn't going to be the first Stewart to shirk,' Henry Fonda recounted. As a result, he did not want the studio to bail him out. Jim is just like that.'

Before attempting to join, Jim and Olivia de Havilland travelled to Houston in August 1940, along with Henry Fonda, Tyrone Power, and numerous other celebrities, to play at a fundraiser for the British war effort at the Houston Coliseum. 'Jim and I had created a magic performance to perform,' Fonda recounted. I use the term "perfected" loosely, because when the tricks went wrong, it didn't matter. We were having a great time, and so was the audience. We returned for an encore, and I played the cornet as best I could, while Jim played his reliable accordion. It was worthwhile because we raised more than $100,000.'

Stewart received his Army physical in November 1940, but he was rejected because he weighed ten pounds less than the War Department's standard for a man of his height.

'Jim was distraught when they refused him,' Burgess Meredith explained. 'I told him that if all he wanted was ten pounds, all he had to do was eat a high-fat diet. Worse, the press had uncovered his rejection and was blasting unpleasant headlines all over the place about being a movie hero who was too lightweight for Uncle Sam. That really devastated him.'

Jim recalls his father calling him after reading one of those headlines. "'I'm coming out to Hollywood," Dad stated over the phone. I'm going to hit a few of those reporters in the nose. We'll file legal action against them." "Dad, that won't help at all," I said. You cannot treat the press in this manner. It will only make matters worse." "Then we'll hire a public-relations guy," he added. I'll hire the best in the industry." "No, Dad," I responded. Simply leave well alone." Of fact, my father was only letting me know that he was on my side. He was saying, "You've got nothing to be ashamed of, son." That made me happy.'

He followed Meredith's instructions and ate two spaghetti dishes per day, along with whatever else he could fit in. 'He stuck with it for four months,' Meredith recounted, 'and I could tell he was becoming heavier.' Stewart, on the other hand, insisted that his diet did not cause him to gain weight.

The Philadelphia Story premiered to excellent acclaim at Radio City Music Hall in the autumn of 1940. According to the New York Herald Tribune, "Stewart contributes the majority of the comedy." His attitude to a snooty culture based on riches is hilarious. In addition, he provides some of the most enticing love moments in the film.' The Hollywood Reporter stated, 'There are simply not enough superlatives to adequately appreciate this program.' The Philadelphia Story, which was released nationwide in December, continued to make money wherever it was screened. The news spread quickly throughout Hollywood that the picture will be nominated for an Academy Award.

During the last weeks of 1940 and into January 1941, Jim made three pictures in fast succession: Come Live With Me and Ziegfeld Girl for his home studio MGM, and Pot o' Gold for United Artists. In 1941, they were all issued in fast succession.

Stewart starred as a penniless writer who meets an attractive immigrant, Hedy Lamarr, who has fled her Nazi-occupied country in Come Live With Me. He offers to marry her in exchange for a weekly payment so that she can become a US citizen. He is also motivated to create a novel about his position, which he sends to a publisher, oblivious to the fact that his new wife is the publisher's mistress. She has fallen out of love with the publisher and into love with her husband at the end of the film.

Ziegfeld Girl was an elaborate musical directed by Robert Z Leonard, with musical parts by Busby Berkeley. It starred Judy Garland, Lana Turner, and Hedy Lamarr, three of the studio's biggest female stars. Stewart played Lana Turner's boyfriend in what was really a supporting role, but he received top billing since he had become such a great star. The movie was one of MGM's biggest hits in 1941.

In Pot o' Gold, Jim played a music store manager who, with the help of Paulette Goddard, helps a struggling band achieve radio stardom. Stewart described the picture as "easily the worst film I ever made." 'I just couldn't bring myself to view that movie until 1950, when I was staying in a hotel in New York,' he recalled. When I switched on the television, there was this terrible film playing.'

Pot o' Gold and Ziegfeld Girl were shot concurrently. 'That was a crazy period,' Jim said. In the morning, I'd work on one film, then in the afternoon, I'd work on another. I had no idea where I was. When I arrived at MGM one day, I discovered that Lana Turner's character had died. "You'll have to remind me," I said to the director. "Did I murder Lana?"

Jim was overjoyed to find that he had been nominated for an Oscar for his role in The Philadelphia Story, but he didn't expect to win: 'The funny thing is, I never thought my performance in that picture was all that good. I was confident that my performance in Mr. Smith was superior. And I knew Fonda's performance in The Grapes of Wrath was superior to my performance in Philadelphia Story. In fact, I voted for Hank and told him about it about a week before the awards.'

'You're going to win it,' Fonda said to Jim.

'No, can't see how,' Jim responded. People probably think I'm terrific at portraying newspapermen.'

'One thing is certain,' Fonda replied. 'I'm not going to be there. You know how I feel about the Oscars. It's not the losing that bothers me. When you win, you get the "Oh no, not him" gasps. So I'm leaving town till everything is over.'

'What are your plans?'

'I'm sailing away with John Ford. Let's go to Mexico. 'Let's go fishing.'

'I, too, do not want to attend the awards. Last year, I felt somewhat humiliated. I'm also quite busy because I'm working on two pictures at Metro. I wish I wasn't working so I could join you on your fishing trip. Have a safe journey, Hank.'

'So I decided not to go,' Jim explained. Then I got a call from someone at the Motion Picture Academy asking if I was going to the ceremony. I blurted out, "Wall, I'm really busy at the studio and . . ." "Look, Mr. Stewart, I'm just checking on all the nominees," he explained. But I hope you'll be able to make it. 'I believe it would be in your best interests to attend.'That puzzled me because that was the year the Academy tried really hard to keep all of the results hidden. That was the year they started using sealed envelopes with the winners' names inside. Nobody was meant to know who had won what. So I couldn't tell if this person knew something and wanted to make sure I was there, or if he just wanted to make sure all the nominees were there. But it appeared to me that he was attempting to tell me something. I had no idea. But I figured I should go to the awards... just in case.'

It was just as well, for he was nominated Best Actor at the Oscars ceremony on February 27, 1941. The film's only other Oscar was for a script by Donald Ogden Stewart. Ginger Rogers, Jim's ex-girlfriend, beat Katharine Hepburn to the role of Kitty Foyle, which Hepburn had turned down. However, Hepburn in The Philadelphia

Story is remembered more than Ginger Rogers in Kitty Foyle.

Fonda congratulated Jim via telegram. Alex had received the news and called his son in Indiana. 'My father responded, 'I hear you received some type of prize,' Jim recounted. What kind of award?" "It's called a Best Actor Award," I said. Every year, they distribute them. This year, I won for The Philadelphia Story. "Have you seen that?" "Never mind about that," he said. "How does your prize appear?" "It's a statuette of a man with a sword," I explained. It appears to be gold, but it is not. It's known as an Oscar." "Well," answered the man, "whatever they call it, send it over so I can put it on show in the store." So I sent it to my father, and the Oscar was on display in a glass case in the hardware store.'

Stewart reported for a second physical a few days after winning the Oscar. 'Bill Grady took me out of the studio. "Why don't you just run a whole test on me and forget to weigh me?" I approached the officer in charge. "But that would be irregular," he remarked. So I reminded him, "Wars are also irregular." But there will undoubtedly be a battle." And the officer administered the test without weighing me. I ran outside, found Bill sitting in his car, and just exclaimed, "I'm in! I'm in!"'

Louis B. Mayer tried once more to convince Stewart out of enrolling. 'Mayer was just so desperate to say something that would dissuade me from enlisting,' Jim remembered. He even stated that America would never be drawn into the war. He went on to say, "You're just giving up this wonderful screen career you've made for yourself, and all you'll be doing is sitting at some clerk's desk on a military base somewhere, and then you'll regret what you're doing." I replied to myself, "Mr. Mayer, this country's conscience is bigger than all the studios in Hollywood put together, and the time will come when we'll have to fight." He threw up his hands after about an hour of disputing the subject with me and remarked, "You're just a bull-headed fella from Philadelphia." I didn't want to correct him and tell him I was from Pennsylvania, so I simply answered, "Mr. Mayer, you better believe it."

'The next thing he did was announce a large farewell party for me, and every star at the studio was invited. I knew it was a publicity stunt--and I was right--because he had the public relations staff spread the narrative that Metro-Goldwyn-Mayer was happy to have one of its biggest actors enlist in the Air Force. That was a huge party. And the majority of the celebrities that attended came because they wanted to say farewell, not because they were told to. There were a lot of actors there, some of whom I only knew superficially and had never worked with, but they all wanted to salute me with encouraging words and even some patriotic enthusiasm. I could tell who the performers were who would enlist when the time came.

'"You know you're throwing away your career, don't you?" Clark Gable said to me. "Yep, I know," I answered. He went on to say, "You won't catch me doing that, but I wish you Godspeed." Wall . . . When his wife Carole [Lombard] was killed in a plane crash while touring to raise bonds for the war effort, Gable didn't waste a second joining in the Air Force... and he didn't put himself out of harm's way. He was right in the middle of it, flying aboard American bombers and getting shot at. He put his life in danger. So please don't tell me I'm the only one who put everything on the line.' Rosalind Russell was in attendance. She brought out a handkerchief and wiped away every trace of lipstick left on my face by the actresses. She slowly cleaned away each little crimson mark, and beneath each one, she wrote the name of the actress whose stain it was. I kept that handkerchief with me for the rest of the war as a good luck charm.'

When he wound up in the hospital just a few days before reporting for duty, he realised he needed all the luck he could conjure. 'Jim was flying in his little plane [a Stinson 105] when his engine started to stall,' Burgess Meredith recounted. He made a forced landing, but landed with such a thud that he was beaten around and barely remained awake. I went to see him in the hospital, where he had been for a few days. He had a baseball-sized bump on his skull and cuts on his face, but he was sitting up and smiling. "Jim, are you sure you can survive a war?" I said. You're struggling just to stay alive in your own plane." "It's not a matter of survival," he explained. It's all about doing the right thing." I couldn't tell if he was scared or not. He never wore his heart on his sleeve.'

On March 22, 1941, James Stewart reported for duty. The Pacific Electric Company was the pickup location. 'There were all the guys who were about to be inducted, and Jim was thrilled to lose himself in the crowd,' said Burgess Meredith. There were hundreds of fathers, mothers, brothers, and sisters crying and celebrating, as well as hundreds of UCLA students wearing World War I German helmets and ridiculing the Nazis with songs and signs. It reminded me of a carnival or the start of a major Saturday college football game.'

Jim boarded the vehicle with the other recruits and was taken to an induction centre in Los Angeles, where he was given the name Private James Stewart. MGM's publicity department dispatched news cameramen and photographers to capture every scene. Jim smiled for the cameras but was upset that his celebrity was being used against him. 'I could tell all the other males felt they needed to keep their distance from me,' he explained. 'I was suddenly the world's loneliest private. 'I just wanted to be one of the guys.' At Fort McArthur, where we were stationed, there were no photographers. When we first had a mail call, the sergeant lined us up and handed out our letters one by one, so if you had 10 letters, you had to march up to him ten times. Most guys had four or five letters, but I had-oh, I don't know-a slew of fan letters that the studio persisted in forwarding to me. So I was marching back and forth to the sergeant... and I had a sore thumb. But I made a point of making jokes about it to whoever I happened to be standing in line with, such as "Another tax bill from Uncle Sam" or "Got a letter here from a cousin in Europe who says the Germans are peeing in their pants 'cos they heard us Yanks might be coming." And it let the other soldiers relax around me, and before we knew it, we were all simply enlisted men facing an uncertain future.'

Private Stewart was deployed to an Army Air Corps unit at Moffett Field after five days at Fort McArthur. When word got out about James Stewart's whereabouts, crowds of female fans and press photographers flocked to Moffett Field, hoping to catch a glimpse of the actor in uniform. Jim chose to stay in camp for the first few weeks to avoid them, declining every overnight pass. Meanwhile, his fellow trainees took advantage of any opportunity to escape out of camp, frequently leaving Jim on his own.

'It was a sort of mass panic,' he explained. 'I suppose it had something to do with someone prominent being in uniform. "You can't give up your overnight pass with all those girls out there waiting for you," one of the guys stated. You may choose any of them." "One girl would be fine," I responded. But there are a hundred of 'em... and I wouldn't put money on my survival." So I just stayed on post for a few weeks till the uproar subsided and everyone forgot about me.' Or so he had assumed.

Stewart was promoted to corporal and assigned the responsibility of drill training within a few weeks. He was classified as an aviation officer candidate within a few months. However, neither the general public nor MGM had forgotten about James Stewart, and a flood of requests for interviews with Jim came on the commanding officer's desk. When Jim persisted on not being interviewed, his commanding officer issued a blanket ban on all members of the media.

Jim wasn't sure he'd be left alone, but he was--but only because the MGM publicity staff went into overdrive that summer of 1941, sending stories allegedly written by Stewart to magazines and newspapers. 'It was really embarrassing to have my name on headlines describing what it was like to be a movie star living on a meagre salary and prepping for war,' he said. 'I attempted to stop it, but it was in my contract that the publicity department could write whatever they wanted and put my name on it,' she says. It made me realise that if I returned to acting after leaving the Air Force, there would be some adjustments in my contract.'I was instructed to write an essay in which I stated that the topic of debate in my barracks was whether Deanna Durbin's new spouse was right for her or not. Of course, Deanna was a major MGM star, and the story was meant to promote her... not that she had anything to do with it. Apparently, I told my army buddies that her spouse was unquestionably deserving of her.'

The MGM press kit did not fool everyone. 'If the Metro press department doesn't stop these floods of imbecilic, ghost-written letters from Jimmy Stewart, the war department will court martial him on the grounds of sabotage,' said Ed Sullavan in the New York Daily Times in August 1941.

According to Burgess Meredith, the temptation to abandon the discipline of army life quickly proved too much for Jim: 'Even a determined guy like Jim couldn't stay faithful to the military all the time. He began seeing an MGM actress, Frances Robinson, and on his day and night passes, he spent his time out of uniform with the girl... that is, he was wearing civilian clothing while off base. Remember that "out of uniform" also meant "out of any type of clothing." For God's sake, he was a dude. When his father arrived from Indiana and discovered that his son was dressed in civilian clothes and going around with an actress, the shit truly hit the fan. Alex inquired as to why Jim had not yet received a commission, and Jim provided some pathetic excuse. The problem was that he'd become a little disoriented. Alex caused such a stir in Jim, and pretty long, Jim had ceased seeing Frances Robinson.'

Stewart hasn't given up on girls entirely. When he had passed, he went to the home of Leland Hayward and Margaret Sullavan, where he met singer Dinah Shore. Jim and Dinah were soon a couple, and it was evident to those closest to them that the two were in love.

Despite having given his heart to Dinah, he was able to refocus his efforts on the Air Force. He completed the academic prerequisites and successfully completed a test flight, earning him his wings and promotion to second lieutenant. On December 7, 1941, as he was waiting for his commission, which was scheduled in January, the Japanese destroyed Pearl Harbour, and America entered the war.

The War Department now put pressure on James Stewart to use his reputation to help the war cause. On December 15, Jim appeared on a radio program with Edward G Robinson, Walter Brennan, Orson Welles, Walter Huston, Lionel Barrymore, and a slew of other Hollywood stars. We Hold These Truths, which aired across all networks, commemorated the 150th anniversary of the Bill of Rights.

Jim obtained his commission in January 1942. Expecting to devote all of his efforts and energies to the Air Force, he was surprised when the War Department ordered him to make regular appearances on a radio show with ventriloquist Edgar Bergen in which the dummy Charlie McCarthy displayed overt patriotism by signing up for all branches of the American armed forces over a three-month period. 'That was a huge disgrace for Jim,' Burgess Meredith recalled. 'All he wanted to do was go back to his Air Force job, but he couldn't get away from being an actor. He began to worry if the Air Force would allow him to fight. That disturbed him a lot.'

His notoriety earned him an invitation to the White House in January 1942, to celebrate President Roosevelt's birthday. He was honoured to do one special job as a film star in February: he presented his pal Gary Cooper with an Oscar for Best Actor for his role in Sergeant York.

In March, he was summoned back into the spotlight for a radio play called Letter at Midnight. He portrayed a soldier sending a letter to explain to his family why he felt it was so vital for him to enrol. A month later, he narrated Winning Your Wings, a recruitment film in which he was forced to warn the young men in the audience, 'Consider the influence these glittering wings have on the women.'

'I had to do a lot of morale-boosting stuff in films and on radio,' Jim explained, 'and while I knew it was essential, I truly was beginning to feel I'd never get off the ground as a pilot.'

In July, he reunited with Cary Grant and Katharine Hepburn for a Lux Radio Theatre production of The Philadelphia Story, the ultimate objective of which was to encourage people to buy war bonds. 'Jim was anxious that he wouldn't get into the war, and he whined to me and everyone else, including Leland Hayward,' said Burgess Meredith. So Hayward contacted General Kenneth McNaughton, who was involved in Hayward's Thunderbird Field project, and informed him of Jim's concern; the General instantly moved Jim.'

Lieutenant James Stewart was transferred to Kirkland Field in New Mexico, near Albuquerque, to train bombardier pilots seventeen months after his entrance. 'I discovered, for the first time since putting on my uniform, that I finally felt free of that part of myself that was an actress,' Jim explained. 'Most people still thought I was James Stewart from the movies... but they had to overlook that, especially if I outranked them.'For a long time, I struggled with the fact that I was older than most of my superiors... as well as many of the guys in my rank. That made me feel elderly... and I was only 34 years old! Then I realised I was doing nothing but training pilots when all I wanted to do was do the job I was trained for... fly the bombers and... wall, just do the job. So I requested a transfer.'

His move was accepted in December 1942, and he found himself at

Hobbs Field, also in New Mexico, where he began serious training to pilot a Flying Fortress. 'Flying the bomber wasn't an issue for me,' he explained. 'It was learning all the technicalities of navigation that I struggled with because I was never good at maths. As a result, I had to work harder than other people. The young lads... they could solve a navigational difficulty in a matter of minutes, but it took me more than an hour.'

Despite his difficulties, he completed all of the needed examinations and was moved to Salt Lake City in February 1943 with thirty other newly trained pilots to receive their assignments to various air groups. 'When I graduated as a B-17 commander, I was stranded in Salt Lake City while everyone else got their assignments.' 'What's the hold-up?' he approached his superior commander.

Jim delivered what may have been a passionate and angry monologue from one of his films when instructed to be patient. 'I understand what's going on. Someone is preventing me from joining the battle because they are scared I will be killed, and then someone will have to explain how they killed James Stewart, the movie star. I'm no better or worse than any other pilot you've got. No, not at all. I'm better than most of your pilots, and I want to do the job Uncle Sam has paid me to do. Everyone knows that the Pacific War is snatching every pilot as soon as he can fly, and the same is true in Europe. And anyone in the Air Force who believes the Japanese or German air forces will hit Idaho is insane!'

His tirade had little impact other than to enrage his superior commander. 'If you talk like that to me again, I'll demote you,' said the CO.

'Wall, I felt I'd made quite a speech but... I didn't appear to make much of an impression since I found myself sitting around for a couple more weeks,' Jim remembered. I'll never know if I would have been moved sooner if I hadn't exploded at my commanding officer. Then I was posted to the 29th Group at Gowen Field in Boise [in Idaho], and I knew the war wasn't going to be waged from there.After a week, I became irritated again and complained to my commanding officer. He went on to say, "All I know is, I got orders to classify you as 'static personnel'." That meant exactly what it sounded like. I was trapped there. He went on to say, "From now on, you're an instructor in first-phase training." I wanted to burst out laughing, but I knew that wasn't a good idea, so I kept my lips shut and went about my business.'

But, according to Burgess Meredith, he didn't keep his lips shut completely: 'Jim urged Leland Hayward to find out what or who was holding him back, and Hayward utilised his contacts and found that the Air Force simply had a problem about sending one of America's favourite movie performers off to war.'

With a squadron to train, Stewart soon learned that his assignment in Idaho was not as cushy as he had thought. The winter snow made for perilous conditions. He was saddened when his room-mate, who was also an instructor, was murdered during a takeoff with a trainee pilot at the controls. 'You expect to lose friends and comrades in action,' he told me, 'but to lose someone in training . .. that kind of thing brought you up sharp and made you know that things were gonna get a whole lot worse in war. . . if I ever got into combat.'

While there was a certain amount of teaching Stewart could offer on the ground, much of it could only be done in the air. 'To teach a pilot how to avoid crashing if any of the engines were knocked out, you had to be flying,' he informed me. 'That's when I learned that imparting instruction was not devoid of peril. I had a couple near misses of my own.'

During one night's trip, Jim occupied the co-pilot's seat while a new flight commander took the controls. When the navigator asked to observe how everything functioned in the cockpit, Jim permitted the navigator to occupy his co-pilot's position. Suddenly, the No. 1 engine on the co-pilot's side exploded and the navigator was temporarily blinded by the flash. With the engine on fire, Jim wrestled in the cramped surroundings to haul the navigator out of the co-pilot's seat so he could reach the No. 1 fire extinguisher selection valve. Putting out the fire and gaining control of the bomber, Jim landed the craft successfully.

But not every situation went out so favourably. In one single week, Jim lost three members of his squadron. Barely able to talk about it, he added, 'We were fighting time and the snow, and you know that you've done your best . . . but there's always the nagging sensation you could've done more. You didn't have time to focus on things that went badly.'

Jim would never boast about saving lives, but he confided to Gloria about how he prevented a death on occasions. She told me: 'Jim saved himself and his troops lots of times. When talking about the war to me, he'd say "I was really saving my own skin," but I knew that he thought that the lives of the guys he was educating were his duty. When he lost guys, he felt the weight of that responsibility heavier than ever. But a whole lot more of his troops survived because Jim, who typically seemed to walk through life in slow motion, was as slick as oil when he flew. He'd take over the controls at the last second to escape collisions that would have killed everyone on board. He always allowed the pilots he was training to attempt and get themselves out of difficulty, and only when he sensed, at the very last second, that the pilot wasn't going to perform the trick, Jim took the controls and made an almost instinctual manoeuvre to avert tragedy. There might have been other instructors who would never have permitted their trainee pilots to approach so close to the point of no return, but Jim stated to me, "You had to give them every chance if they were going to have the best chance to survive in actual combat." And a number of his boys did get themselves out of trouble at the last minute. I asked Jim, "Didn't you just want to take over the controls?" And he said, "I wanted to, but I knew I couldn't." He said, "I hope that some of the boys who got themselves out of trouble lived longer in combat because of it." 'He knew he was sending these young guys off to risk their lives, and he knew there was a high mortality rate among pilots and crew. But he had to push that out of his thoughts. His job was to attempt to give them a better opportunity to survive. When he had to let his squadron fly without him, he never left the field tower until all of his planes returned. There were some officers who watched the first few planes of their squadrons come back, and then those officers would depart the tower. But Jim stayed until every last man had returned.'

Although he put his attention on his career, Jim still had time for his romance with Dinah Shore, who managed to keep up with his frequent transfers. Sometimes she would stay at neighbouring hotels, or if Jim had more than just a few days leave, he would return to Los Angeles and stay with Leland Hayward and Margaret Sullavan and pursue his romance with Dinah Shore from there.

Just how serious his relationship with Shore got is something Jim always stayed teasingly unclear about. Joshua Logan stated, 'I heard that he [Jim] wanted to marry Dinah, but he always shrugged it off and said, "I was just kidding people 'cos they kept saying, 'When you gonna get married?'" I never did know what the truth was.'

Burgess Meredith had a feeling he knew something. 'Jim wanted to marry Dinah, and she appeared just as enthusiastic.' Gloria told me, 'If it wasn't for the war keeping Jim and Dinah Shore away, I would never have become Jim's wife, therefore I'm pleased the war kept him open for me.'

In fact, Jim felt that if he was never called up for combat, he would marry Dinah. But, if he was deployed overseas, he determined that the last thing he wanted was a wife who worried about whether her husband would ever return alive. 'Most people in love married because the male wanted to make his girl his wife before the war separated them,' Gloria explained. Jim, on the other hand, took a more pragmatic approach.'

Gloria claimed that years later, when Jim was a raconteur, he recounted an obviously overblown narrative about how he and Dinah decided to drive from Los Angeles to Las Vegas to marry. 'But on the way, Dinah began saying that at nine o'clock they would do such-and-such, and at eleven o'clock they would do such-and-such, and the following morning they would go to some such place, and Jim decided that she had planned their entire future in such minute detail that he simply turned the car around and headed back to Los Angeles.' Jim had no idea Dinah had been seeing actor George Montgomery. She didn't appear to know how to convey the news to Jim.

In June 1943, he was allowed to return to Indiana for his sister Virginia's wedding to a Russian designer, Alexis Alexander Tiranoff. Alexis was an outsider in many ways, and according to Gloria, he had no hope of fitting in with the Stewarts. 'Jim, his father, and the uncles all dubbed Alexis a lightweight; he was just a happy-go-lucky type of chap who never knew where his next job would come from, and Jim said it was typical of Ginnie to marry someone like him because of her dreamy ways. Jim had never realised how similar she was to him in that regard.'

Alexis grew further apart from the Stewarts when he and Ginnie had their first child, a daughter, who was baptised into Alexis' Russian Orthodox religion rather than the Presbyterian faith. A second daughter was likewise not included on the Presbyterian membership records. 'That was a cardinal sin to Jim's father,' Gloria explained. 'Alex had a short fuse when it came to Alexis and Ginnie until the day Ginnie died.'

Dotie, Jim's other sister, fared much better in her father's eyes. She was artistically skilled and admirably smart; she embodied her father's ideal of a young lady. 'She was also a very down-to-earth girl,' Gloria remarked. She travelled to New York during WWII to work in the graphics department of Mademoiselle magazine, having always wanted to be an artist and illustrator. The American Red Cross utilised several of her drawings as posters, and examples of such posters could be spotted all around Alex's hardware store.

In March 1944, she married one of Jim's former Princeton classmates, Robert Moorehead Perry, who later became a Presbyterian pastor after teaching at New York University. As far as Alex was concerned, he was the ideal son-in-law. Their union resulted in four children.

Chapter 10: Trying to Live a Wonderful Life

Colonel James Stewart boarded the Queen Elizabeth at Portsmouth on August 25, 1945, along with over 15,000 other American servicemen and women returning home, and departed for New York.

Queen Elizabeth arrived five days later. As the men and women disembarked, popular bands, rather than military bands, played swing music. Colonel Stewart refused to leave the ship first, despite the fact that his family and friends were waiting for him at the St Regis Hotel in Manhattan. He insisted on seeing every soldier, sailor, nurse, and airman off personally.

'It was a fantastic day,' he recalled. 'This fantastic music was being played by Cab Calloway and Sammy Kaye [and their bands]. Glenn Miller, it was stated, would have been there if he was still alive. I just wanted to enjoy every moment, so I went first to see who else was getting off the ship. When I eventually made it onshore, I was hoarse and my hand ached from saluting thousands of times. There's a saying about living in the now. I didn't want the experience to end. Then I went to a downtown hotel to meet my family and several friends who were waiting for me. That was... by golly... that was simply something filled with emotion... and it was... it was just a private thing for me.' 'My father insisted on holding a parade in my honour in Indiana. My father was generally right, but not this time. I didn't want to be thought of as a hero. There were many other heroes--true heroes--who deserved that honour. Going home was a private matter for me.'

Despite his desire for quiet, he couldn't escape James Stewart's public image, and whether he wanted it or not, he was being viewed as a hero. It was mostly a matter of executing a public relations obligation when he had to attend the next day at a press conference at Major General Clarence Kells' office in Brooklyn.

He was asked if he intended to resume his cinematic career. 'I'm just not a young fella anymore,' he replied. (He was only 37 years old.) 'I believe I'd only be suitable for playing Mickey Rooney's grandad.'

When asked if he would appear in any war films, Jim stated that he would be unlikely to appear in any Second World War films. He also kept his word. His reasons for refusing all attempts to cast him in the innumerable war pictures made throughout the 1950s and 1960s were very personal,' he explained. 'I am proud of my combat record, and I have respect for every warrior who lived and died fighting for freedom,' he told me in the late 1980s. And every deceased woman. I believe it would have been disrespectful to those men and women if I had made a film about the war and it turned out to be a lousy film. No one sets out to make a terrible movie... yet they can all come out bad... so I wouldn't take the chance. And I resolved without hesitation that I would never abuse my own role in the conflict for the purpose of a film. That would be disgusting.'

While Jim dismissed the possibility of making war photographs, he understood he couldn't bet on making any kind of picture. He was conscious that, like many others in his situation, a film career might not be in his future. 'There were a number of us [Hollywood actors] who had participated in the war, and when we got back, there was a whole new generation of prominent performers who had kind of stolen our places,' Henry Fonda recounted. Some of the guys who were big stars before the war returned looking like hell. Clark Gable experienced something similar. He appeared to be ten years older. Jim [Stewart] has also aged significantly. Gregory Peck and Van Johnson were among the newcomers. But, in the end, it wasn't so horrible. Those of us on contract with major studios were welcomed back. Louis B. Mayer nearly died with joy when he reclaimed Clark Gable. He thought he had Jim back, but Jim had already made other plans.'

When Jim enlisted in 1941, he still had eighteen months left on his

MGM contract. Leland Hayward had retired as an agent to focus on creating Broadway productions. He sold MCA his whole client list, which included Jim. However, Hayward remained Jim's friend, and he informed Jim that the time he had left with MGM had, in reality, continued to run after his enlistment. That's why Jim had to perform all the press MGM threw at him after enlisting. And it meant that his contract had officially expired eighteen months after he enlisted.

Hayward advised Jim to avoid any additional exclusive contracts because the old star system was crumbling. Non-exclusive arrangements were being made with new stars; in fact, Hayward had initiated the trend by signing one of his most recent clients, Gregory Peck, to many non-exclusive contracts. Peck was allowed to work at almost every major studio, which meant that no studio could 'loan' him out. When one studio paid Peck for his services, no other studio could profit from it. Peck received the whole amount paid by the studio, excluding agent expenses.

Jim visited with Louis B Mayer in September 1945, who welcomed him back to the studio like a long-lost son. 'Mr. Mayer was extremely good at being my father... until I informed him I wasn't coming back to work at his studio,' Jim remembered. He then claimed I was the son of a different kind of father. Then I remember him breaking down in tears and... wall, that was just pitiful. When he realised it wasn't going to work, he informed me that they had already prepared my first major return film... in which I would play an air ace. That was it for me, Wall. I could tell he was going to use my military record against me, so I told him there was nothing else I could say. But he had something more to say... "You'll never work again." "You know what, Mr. Mayer?" I said. "I'm not sure I want to be an actor anymore." And for a little minute, I contemplated it.'

Johnny Swope and Burgess Meredith had left the Brentwood house to start new lives with their new wives--Swope to Dorothy McGuire and Meredith to Paulette Goddard. That meant Jim had no place to reside.

Alex wished Jim would return to Indiana. Jim tried to persuade him that if he resided in Indiana, he would be unable to make films in Hollywood. 'Make these movie creators come out to Indiana and make their movies here,' Alex remarked.

Jim carefully explained that none of the studios were planning to relocate to Indiana anytime near. 'Why not?' Alex wondered. 'You've won one of those Oscars. That elevates you to a position of prominence in Hollywood. Speak with them. Inform them that Indiana is an excellent location for filming. Tell them we have your Oscar displayed in the store front.'

Jim had a difficult time convincing Alex that Hollywood would not follow him down to Indiana just because he had an Oscar. 'They give out Oscars every year, Dad,' he explained. 'In Hollywood, there are hundreds of Oscars. In Indiana, there is only one.'

'Yes,' Alex responded, 'but it's arguably the most important Oscar in the world.'

Jim was rescued by Henry Fonda. Jim was invited to live with him, his wife Frances, and their two children, Jane and Peter. 'We had a wonderful house in the hills with a modest outbuilding that I had built for my children,' Fonda explained. 'It was their playhouse, so Jim lived in it for three months.'

'It had everything I needed,' Jim remembered of the playhouse. It was furnished with a bed, a tiny kitchen, and a bathroom. Hank didn't just build a playhouse when he built it. It was a genuine article. Small, yet very real. I'm not sure how Peter and Jane reacted when I kicked them out of their playhouse... Hank still had a thing for cats. They were crowding the playhouse.'

Hank and Jim would spend their evenings in the playhouse, building model aeroplanes and listening to jazz music. Jim arrived in town for Christmas and agreed to assist Hank in convincing Peter, who was just six at the time, that Santa Claus was real. 'I suppose it was the first Christmas after I came home from England... and Peter didn't believe in Santa,' Jim recalled. So Hank told me, "You've got to help me make him believe Santa is real." I responded by saying, "I suppose you expect me to dress up as Santa and climb on the roof." "That's exactly what you have to do," he added.

'Hank and Frances had been gracious enough to allow me to stay there... cathouse or playhouse--it was kind of both. Anyway, I dressed up as Santa and climbed on the roof, stomping around, while Hank was inside convincing Peter that Santa was on the roof. I was getting into character, saying "Ho! Ho! Ho!" and walking up and down... then I slipped and almost fell off the roof. Hank later told me, "You almost fell off." "Good thing I didn't," I said. "I'll say it's lucky," he said. "How would I have told my son that Santa had fallen off the roof?" "You will be Santa next year," I said. He didn't give it any thought.'

For a period, Jim tried to relive his pre-war Hollywood experience by attending parties and dating young girls. Kirk Douglas spoke of a party he attended shortly after arriving in Hollywood with a young German girl whom his agent had set him up with in his memoirs The Ragman's Son. Jimmy Stewart, Hank and Frances Fonda were also present. According to Douglas, Frances pulled the young German actress away for a brief conversation and giggled. The actress informed Douglas that she needed to use the restroom. As Douglas waited for his date to return, people began to leave the party. After a half-hour delay, he discovered she had gone with Jim and the Fondas; Kirk assumed Frances had persuaded her to accompany Jim.

'I asked Jim about it, and he claimed he didn't remember Kirk Douglas, who was almost unknown at the time, at any party,' Gloria, who uncovered the anecdote in Kirk Douglas's book, informed me during one of our transatlantic phone talks. But he claimed that Frances Fonda was always bringing him ladies to date, and it's possible that she loved the look of Kirk's girl and convinced her to dump Kirk for Jim. But Jim had no idea he'd ever taken one of Kirk's dates. And he didn't need Frances to find him girls because he could do it himself. However, Jim may have lost interest in partying and going out with a lot of girls by that point. He'd changed since the war, or he'd just started acting his age. That's why Frances took it upon herself to locate his girlfriends, despite his repeated warnings.'

Jim had almost stopped coming to parties by early 1946. He was sick of the Hollywood lifestyle and preferred to stay at home, grill with Henry Fonda, and make model aeroplanes. 'I think he came back to Hollywood and attempted to take up where he had left off, but the war changed him-no doubt,' Fonda said. When I asked him how he was feeling, he replied, "I'm feeling that so much is just so... superficial." "Are you unhappy?" I inquired. "No, I'm very happy," he replied. However, in a different way." He began visiting his family in Indiana more frequently. He went on and on about his father. Alex would berate him for not attending church every week. Jim had never been to church on a regular basis in the time I'd known him... but he was the most--not religious fella--but the fella with the greatest faith I'd ever known.Alex, of course, desired that he give up acting and return home to handle the store. But Jim had not given up. I believe he'd simply witnessed the worst of humanity, as many of us had, and Jim took it to heart. He'd matured. I wish I could have! But he was still a boy when he was with me, building kit planes. We didn't have to converse in order to have a conversation. We mostly sat on the floor with all these aeroplane and plane parts, and it was, "I've got part C, which fits into the slot in part F." And you say, "I've got parts A, B and G, what parts have you got?" That was all Jim and I needed to forget about movies. But I could tell he was worried about his job; no one was willing to hire him.'He also mentioned how all of his buddies were married and had families, but he remained single. He kept complaining about being old, and I told him, "You're not even forty, for Christ's sake." "Yeah," he admitted, "but I feel old." That's what the war did to some guys. So I kept forcing him to build planes.'

Jim left the playhouse and returned to Brentwood. But, until he married Gloria in 1949, he spent Christmas Eve with the Fondas, relishing the pleasure of waking up on Christmas morning and seeing the children open their presents. 'Jim liked coming over and helping put up the tree,' Fonda added. 'We had a lovely tall tree, and because Jimmy was the tallest, the kids assigned him the task of placing the star on top. He still needed to climb a ladder to get there, but the ladder wobbled, Jim crashed against the tree, and he just rode the tree all the way down. It looked like something from a cartoon. It ruined the tree, but it was the most amusing thing.'

As the new year of 1946 approached, Jim began to worry if any film offers would come his way. Mayer's forecast that he'd never work again appeared to be coming true. Fonda had just landed his first film role since 1943's The Ox-Bow Incident. John Ford was going to direct My Darling Clementine for 20th Century-Fox, and Fonda (not John Wayne, Ford's favourite performer) was going to play Wyatt Earp. Then Jim learned that Darryl F Zanuck, production chief at 20th Century-Fox, wanted him to play Doc Holliday, the second main character.

'I think Zanuck's notion to portray Jim as Doc Holliday was a stroke of genius,' Fonda said in 1976. Nobody else, least of all Ford, saw Jim in the role, although he would've been fantastic. He's a true actor's actor, and he would have made everyone forget about Mr. Smith and Destroy. But Ford refused to think Jim could play the part. So, who did he end up with? Victor Mature is a kind and professional individual. And he was actually rather terrific in the role. He was never, however, the outstanding actor Jim is. Mature confesses he's not an actor. He's said it before and will say it again: "I'm no actor, and I've got all the films to prove it." One of John Ford's worst blunders was not casting Jim.'

According to Fonda, Ford may be "short on vision, despite what everyone says." Of course, Fonda was biassed; he and Ford had a falling out during the filming of Mr. Roberts in 1955 and never spoke again. But, if Jim had played Doc Holliday, it would have been a piece of screen history, bringing together James Stewart and Henry Fonda for the first time in a film that is unquestionably one of the great Westerns. (Fonda claimed that after their dispute, Ford retaliated by casting Jim in three films: Two Rode Together, The Man Who Shot Liberty Valance, and Cheyenne Autumn.)

In the end, a film came Jim's way in 1946. In the short term, it was one of Jim's biggest flops, but in the long run, it was the film for which he was best remembered. Frank Capra's It's a Wonderful Life was the film.

'Frank called me and said that he had an idea for a movie and asked if I'd come over,' Jim recalled the afternoon Capra pitched his idea to him. So I approached him and he began telling me about this film. "You're a fella in a small town, you see, and you're not doing very well," he explained. You want to help people... you want to do something for your wife... but everything is going wrong. And then you attempt suicide... Frank is now slowing down as he hears himself telling this story. "And you try to commit suicide by jumping off a bridge into a river, and an angel named Clarence... and I could see the horror on his face, but he kept going. "Clarence hasn't won his wings yet so he jumps into the water to save you, but he can't swim and you save him." Wall... he finished... he paused... and I didn't say anything because I was waiting for him to say something else... and he said, "It doesn't sound too good, does it?" Wall, I believed in Frank and told him, "Frank, if you want to do a movie about an angel named Clarence who hasn't won his wings, I'm your man."'

Jim was, in fact, the man-George Bailey, a small-town citizen who has reached a point of desperation after all of his plans have failed, leaving him financially ruined and facing disgrace. Fortunately, Heaven sends Clarence (played by Henry Travers) to show George the value of his life. The film then retells George's life, highlighting all of the good he has done. Mr. Potter (played by Lionel Barrymore) is a ruthless banker who becomes his undoing. The Christmas sequence, in which George wishes he had never been born, is the film's high point. He learns that no one in his hometown knows who he is because he hasn't been born. The young brother whose life he saved is no longer alive. All of the people whose lives he had enriched are now in some form of misery. He decides he wants to live after all, and Clarence returns everything to its original state. And, because it is Christmas on the day George is emotionally and spiritually saved, a miracle occurs when the townspeople arrive at his house, having collected enough money to save him financially in exchange for everything he has done for them.

It's a Wonderful Life began filming on April 8, 1946. It was Jim's first film in five years, and he was nervous at first, but he rejected the rumours that had circulated for years that he floundered at the start of production. 'It's like riding a bike,' he says. 'You never forget how to do it, but if you don't do it for a long time, you might be a little shaky at first. 'I was a little shaky, I guess, but nothing like the befuddled actor who has been discussed over the years.'Lionel Barrymore allegedly took me aside and lectured me. He never did anything like that. He did notice a couple of times that I was just regaining my sound-stage legs, and he'd just say something encouraging.'

Donna Reed, who played George Bailey's wife, confirmed Jim's story. 'Jimmy isn't a man who lacks confidence, and he didn't lack confidence when we started filming It's a Wonderful Life,' she told me. He occasionally asked Frank Capra if he could re-enact a scene, and Frank always agreed, and Jimmy was soon in full flow.Like everyone else, I thought he was a wonderful person. He was always courteous and considerate to others. The only thing that surprised me was how much he preferred to be alone. I expected him to be outgoing. But he seemed at ease being alone. He'd occasionally sit on the set and read a comic book. He appeared to be lost in thought at times. I often wanted to approach him and ask him what he was thinking, but I thought it would be too intrusive. I tried some sneaky psychology on him one day and said, "George Bailey has seen wonderful times and terrible times." Do you find something in your own life that helps you feel that way when you play him at his lowest ebb?" And he added, "I've never felt anything like George in my life." I'm content with my life. I don't have anything to complain about."But I did learn, thanks to Frank Capra, that he didn't like talking about the war. But many of the men who returned from the war felt the same way; they didn't want to talk about it. So I don't think it was the war that drove him to his quiet little corner. "Aw, Jim's a loner," Henry Fonda once said to me. He prefers to be alone. You don't have to be concerned about him. He's happy." And I suppose that sums up Jimmy Stewart: he's content.'

Capra believed that, while Jim was content, he had an underlying sense of being as close to the edge as anyone could ever be'. 'Jim likes to keep a lot of himself beneath the surface of his skin,' Capra explained. And every now and then, he gets a part that brings those hidden qualities to the surface. Many of Jim's characters, such as George Bailey and Mr. Smith, are men who appear to be on the verge of insanity at times. That doesn't mean Jim is insane; far from it. However, when Jim plays those roles, you frequently see something quite frightening. He can play a man on the verge of breaking down better than any other actor I've seen. And the man must be able to find that somewhere deep within himself in order to play it. It's evident in many of Jim's performances, not just Bailey and Smith--though Bailey and Smith are excellent examples.'

It is undeniable that Jim touched on a dark subject in many of his performances over the course of his career. Many people envision a typical James Stewart role as a man who is always calm, gentle, humorous, and amiable--in fact, they envision the type of character he would come to play in Harvey (1950). However, his role in Harvey was that of a man who is far from normal and sane. Mr. Smith and George Bailey were ordinary men thrust into extraordinary circumstances. What we see on screen is James Stewart losing control of the situation, and when he does, he often appears to be a man going insane. He even admitted that it was the only way he knew to play those men:

'An actor uses the tools with which he was born: his body and his thoughts. My mind, like everybody else's, is considerably more sophisticated than anyone would care to admit. I've discovered that several of my films have given me the opportunity to let go of something that has been building up inside of me. The issue is, when you're performing, everything is under controlled settings, so I'm not going insane... though others may believe otherwise. I don't get caught up in a role. I only live it when I'm doing it. But if I appear out of control, as my characters frequently do, especially in [Anthony Mann] Westerns, it's because something I keep under control is allowed to be seen... but it still remains under my control.'

Gloria had as solid an idea as anyone (because no one knew him better): 'I think it's all about his wrath and his ability to manage it almost all of the time. When he plays someone who has had about enough of the world, life, or a particular individual, Jim's wrath explodes through... sometimes like a volcano. I've actually seen him act like that on occasion. What it does for him as an actor--and I've heard him compared to Gary Cooper, for example--is allow him to play a character with a sense of losing all control, whereas Gary Cooper would play the same part as a man who appears, perhaps, more befuddled by it all. Take, for example, High Noon, in which

Coop played a town marshal who seemed perplexed by the town's lack of support. If Jim had played the part--and he could have, despite the fact that it's Coop's best role--he'd display his wrath at the town through gritted teeth and fiery eyes while battling to keep his cool. 'You'd think he'd lose both the gunfight and his sanity in the build-up.'

'If you want to see the genuine Jimmy Stewart, you can find him in It's a Wonderful Life,' Henry Fonda told me. Everything is amplified, but that's as close to the genuine Jim as you can get.'

Perhaps this is why It's a Wonderful Life remains one of Jim Stewart's most popular films among his fans today--they see a glimpse of the genuine James Stewart. It was probably Jim's personal favourite, but for various reasons--though his reasons for appreciating the picture are undoubtedly shared by many, whether or not they are Stewart fans: 'It's my favourite movie. The entire thing was done from a concept, not from a book... not from a play... not from an actual happening... A belief that no one is born to fail. It's as simple as that. That was a good concept.'

If such is the film's charm now, it was completely lost on the 1946 audience. Despite its status as a classic nearly sixty years later, few people found it appealing at the time. It was, in reality, a disaster. When it was opened in December 1946, critics were divided. According to Bosley Crowther of the New York Times, the film's flaw was "its illusory concept of life." Mr. Capra's good people are charming, his small town is pretty enchanting, and his pattern for problem handling is most optimistic and easy... they all reflect theatrical attitudes, rather than normal reality.' Newsweek admitted that it was "far from real life," but it was "so expertly written, directed, and acted that you want to believe it." Variety noted both the good and the bad in the film, stating that "the recounting of this life is just about flawless in its tender and natural element" and that "the ending is slightly overlong and a shade too cloying for all tastes."

Since the film's release, critics have debated its qualities, or lack thereof. According to a 1977 New Yorker review, 'in its own slimy, bittersweet way, it's terribly powerful.'

The fact that the picture was a resounding flop still surprises people today. Despite being nominated for five Oscars, including Best Picture, Best Director, and Best Actor, the film was not well received by the general audience. 'I just don't think that was the type of story people wanted to watch shortly after the war,' Jim explained to me in 1979. They desired a war-related story, such as The Best Years of Our Lives, or a pure piece of slapstick, such as a Red Skelton film. It's only become a classic because of television. I've always despised the idea of television, yet it was the one thing that helped It's a Wonderful Life find an audience. Everyone now believes it was a smash hit. And if people still enjoy the film after all these years, then I, Capra, and everyone else associated with it have done something worthwhile in their lives. But it was a great disappointment for all of us at the moment.'

Jimmy Stewart had filmed his first film since the war, and his career appeared to be in risk. But something more dangerous was emerging, not just for Jim, but for the entire industry.

Chapter 11: The Unknown FBI Agent

Even before America entered the war, James Stewart was aware of the political milieu in Hollywood. The Hollywood Anti-Nazi League openly spoke out against Hitler and the Nazi Party at organized mass rallies at a time when many Americans were isolationists. This pleased many people. To those on the Republican right, such as Stewart, this was an attempt to indoctrinate the American people into Communism. After all, the League's head, scriptwriter Donald Ogden Stewart, was a renowned Communist Party organiser, and many of its members were liberals and lefties. Being a liberal, according to some extreme right-wingers, was just as awful as being on the far left.

Some Americans had adopted Communism as the solution to the faults of capitalism in America since the early 1930s. Many Americans switched to the far left and toyed with Communist beliefs; some stayed left, some shifted to the more liberal centre, while still others shifted to the far right in an attempt to counter Communism's growth in America. By 1934, some in Hollywood were adopting Communism, particularly among screenwriters, who, according to John Wayne, "thought themselves intellectually superior to mere actors, producers, directors, and studio executives."

James Stewart shared Wayne's political convictions because they were both right-wing Republicans, but while Jim was as hostile to Communism as Wayne was, he was less vocal about it. 'Communism was a menace to Hollywood--to America as a whole,' he remarked. 'I just didn't speak at rallies like Duke. 'I did my political speaking at the polling place.'

What Jim wasn't saying was that he was also doing his political speeches behind closed doors and in complete secrecy. He was working undercover for the FBI by 1947, at the specific request of FBI Director J Edgar Hoover.

Gloria didn't know Jim when he first started his covert work. But once they started dating in the summer of 1948, and especially when they married in August 1949, Jim couldn't keep Mary in the dark about his covert mission for the government, and he told her everything. (Whether Jim told Gloria everything before or after their wedding, Gloria never said. But I assume it was before they married, because Stewart was active long before the wedding, and it's inconceivable that he'd join holy matrimony without his wife knowing about his hidden life.)

Jim's services were originally requested by Army Intelligence in early 1947. He was the ideal choice to assist search out subversives in Hollywood since he was both a respected Hollywood actor and an officer in the American Army Air Force Reserve Corps, and he had come from the war as a genuine, highly decorated hero.

'Army Intelligence wants to hire Jim as one of their agents,' Gloria explained. 'But Jim had no desire to be a spy. He had many excellent friends in Hollywood, and he was not pleased with the prospect of spying on them, compiling intelligence reports on them, and reporting back to Army Intelligence. They didn't tell him to do it, and when he said no, they looked to the cave.'

Jim may have assumed that was the end of the matter, but Army Intelligence quickly contacted the FBI, and Jim was soon called to Washington to meet J Edgar Hoover, the FBI's director from 1935 (at the age of forty) until his death in 1972.

'Jim assumed he was going as someone Hoover wanted to shake hands with because of his combat record,' Gloria explained. 'The thing about Jim is that he is a true patriot, so when he received the invitation from Hoover, he was overjoyed. He wanted to shake Hoover's hand and tell him how well the FBI was serving the country.'

Jim met with Hoover and was given a tour of the FBI headquarters. 'Jim was just so impressed and overwhelmed,' Gloria added. 'He saw the FBI as a near-sacred institution. Jim described Hoover as utterly casual, pleasant, polite, and generous. He took Jim to his house for supper, and Jim listened to Hoover talk about his work and the history of the FBI like a fascinated child.'

Jim was hooked after hearing Hoover's sense of self-satisfaction about his crime-fighting exploits. Hoover had been building up to the moment when he would personally approach Stewart for his assistance, and for Jim, being personally requested for assistance by the head of the FBI was almost like a calling from God. 'Jim ran barefoot up the mountain and saw the burning bush--only God's name was J Edgar Hoover,' Gloria said.

Hoover was aware that Jim was uncomfortable with the concept of eavesdropping on his friends and colleagues. He was highly astute in his recruitment of Stewart. 'I know you're a loyal American,' he told Jim. You are a patriot for your country. I know it not only because of your stellar military record, but also because I sensed it today.'

Jim was not frequently impressed by compliments. 'He had learnt that in Hollywood, flattery was what you get when you're on top, and what you don't get when you're on your way down,' Gloria explained. However, this time the statements came from J Edgar Hoover himself. Jim was quickly vowing to do whatever he could to assist the FBI. What Hoover had not immediately admitted was that the FBI needed assistance in locating known and suspected Communists in Hollywood. Jim mistook Hoover's request for assistance in driving the Mafia out of Hollywood for something Jim was more than willing to do.

'When Hoover saw Jim was willing to assist fight crime, he took advantage of it,' Gloria explained. Hoover advised Jim that it was critical to 'fight all forms of evil there are' in Hollywood and throughout America. Jim started talking about people like Bugsy Siegel and Lucky Luciano, who were running rackets in Los Angeles and Las Vegas, and he enthusiastically provided ideas on how to bust them. 'Jim would have done everything to get those criminals out of town,' Gloria explained, "but he was also concerned about how it would all turn out for friends like Cary Grant, who'd developed friendships with some of those people." He wanted to keep his buddies safe, and he told Hoover so.'

Jim told Hoover that he and Cary Grant had held a spectacular party at the Clover Club in New York in February 1947. It was named after Howard Hughes, the pilot who flew the Hercules, a massive seaplane and the largest aircraft ever built. Bugsy Siegel was a guest at the Clover Club. Hoover informed Stewart that the FBI was well aware of Siegel's attendance at the party; the FBI had infiltrated it, in part because they were investigating Hughes. He had been given government funds to create the Hercules as part of the war effort, but it had taken five years to complete at an astounding cost of $18 million--and the war had ended. Hughes' ties to the mob were also known to the government.

Hoover, on the other hand, reassured Jim that anyone who was not actively involved in crime should not be concerned. He went on to emphasise the importance of crusading against everything un-American, and he asked Jim whether he agreed. Gloria stated, 'When Hoover asked Jim that, he could only answer that he did agree.'

The government's fears about subversives' in Hollywood were highlighted by Hoover. He continued to define the government's objective at length, and by the end of his address, he was no longer speaking of "subversives," but of "Communists." Jim agreed with everything Hoover said, and by the time Hoover finished his point, Jim was eager to become engaged. 'But Jim was certain of one thing,' Gloria explained. 'He would not take any type of oath that would make him an official FBI agent, and he would not act as any kind of spy.' He would not, he stated emphatically, "be an informant."

Hoover stated he understood Stewart's worries and agreed that no formal agreement was required between "two American patriots doing their duty." He stated that all he wanted Stewart to do was "talk to people, encourage anyone who might have Communist ideologies to give them up, and get those people to spread the word." 'I think it will take more than a little encouragement to convince those who may be Communists to give it up,' Jim responded.

Hoover agreed, stating the country was "in danger" and that all Americans could have to "fight with whatever weapons are necessary." Jim expressed his understanding and expressed his wish that they could 'fight without drawing blood'. 'Jim said he'd do whatever was necessary,' Gloria explained. The only problem was that Hoover hadn't told him everything.'

For starters, Hoover had no intention of collecting up the Hollywood Mafia. In truth, the FBI's official position was that organised crime did not exist in America. For years, the Mafia got away with murder in the United States, and the cause, many believe, was as evil as the Cosa Nostra itself. It was said that J Edgar Hoover had become compromised by his own greatest secret: he was reputedly a homosexual, and one of the FBI's most sacred rules was that no agent should be a homosexual. Of course, the general public was unaware of Hoover's rumoured secret until after his death in 1972, but the Mafia was well aware, and they purportedly had images of Hoover in compromising poses to prove it. Ironically, due to the Mafia's ties to Hollywood, many Hollywood figures were aware of the rumours that Hoover was gay and that the Mob was blackmailing him. But if this had been offered to Jim, he would have dismissed it as idle chatter. They had said the same thing about him and Fonda. (Among others who insisted in my presence that the gay and blackmailing charges were accurate, and who were in various situations to know--see my book on Frank Sinatra--were movie stars Ava Gardner, Peter

Lawford, and Sammy Davis Jr. It was also asserted by James Cagney, George Raft, and Henry Fonda, as well as a member of Charles 'Lucky' Luciano's Mafia who requested anonymity--see my book The Hollywood Connection.)

The alleged agreement between Hoover and the Mafia was straightforward: the FBI did not pursue organised crime, and the Mob refused to disseminate images of Hoover, particularly those allegedly showing him wearing women's clothing. Only a few Mafia figures were ever imprisoned, including Al Capone for tax evasion and Charles 'Lucky' Luciano for leading a prostitution ring. During WWII, Luciano worked with the OSS (the precursor to the CIA) to arrange the Allied invasion of Sicily, with Luciano's Mafia links in Sicily supporting the Allies. Luciano was released and deported back to Sicily in exchange for his assistance. When he was free, he moved to Cuba to be as near to his American activities as possible.

The FBI saw and reported on the Mafia, but no action was ever done by the Bureau to combat organised crime because it didn't exist officially--Hoover merely denied its existence and refused to investigate it (which later led to Senator Robert F. Kennedy's vigorous investigation of the Mafia). Even as Hoover and Jim talked about rounding up the Mafia bosses in Los Angeles, Hoover knew he had no intention of doing it.

Hoover also failed to inform Jim that the Motion Picture Alliance for the Preservation of American Ideals, which had a sizable membership of Hollywood right-wingers, had invited the House Un-American Activities Committee, or HUAC, to Hollywood. The HUAC had only one goal: to investigate known and suspected Communists. Lists of such people had been compiled, and the HUAC planned to summon them to special hearings to declare their Communist Party membership.

Hoover had already hired a number of Hollywood's right-wing

extremists, including Ronald Reagan, who were given code names. 'Jim refused to have any type of code name, as did a dozen or so others in Hollywood,' Gloria explained. Reagan was particularly active in compiling names of suspected and known Communists.

Hoover was so concerned about the Red Scare in America that he wanted to ensure that his 'Hollywood agents' were not double agents. He instructed Jim to keep a watch on the code-named informers and sent him a list, 'which is how we knew Reagan was one of them,' Gloria claimed. 'But who could have imagined Ronald Reagan was a double agent? It's absurd. But that's what Hoover asked Jim to look into, and Jim did it.'

Jim never uncovered any double agents among the official informers. Hoover then insisted on Jim compiling a list of anybody he suspected of being a Communist. Jim despised the notion, but made 'token efforts,' according to Gloria. People in Hollywood were picking sides, and many on both sides were speaking out loudly. Jim reasoned that drawing conclusions wasn't too difficult. And he had no idea that the HUAC planned to punish some of Hollywood's top stars harshly.

When he was questioned about Frank Capra by the FBI's Los Angeles office, he realised that his findings and allegations were contradictory with the facts. Jim had no idea his pal Capra was a suspected Communist. He also learned that It's a Wonderful Life had been a HUAC target. The Committee claimed that the picture was 'un-American' because its villain was a ruthless banker who, according to the HUAC, represented capitalist America. The fact that the film depicted its hero, Stewart, as a banker who utilised money for good did not appear to have impressed the witch-hunters. Capra's earlier films, Mr. Deeds Goes to Town and You Can't Take It With You, were likewise criticised for implying that capitalism was wicked. Then there came Mr. Smith Goes to Washington, which dared to insinuate that there was corruption in the American Senate.

When Jim discovered this, he reported to HUAC that Capra was no more a Communist than he was. They informed Jim that Army Intelligence had compiled a lengthy file on Capra, chronicling the director's Communist activities since 1932, and that the HUAC had granted him access to it. Capra was claimed to have signed the Communist Party election petition in 1932. Capra confirmed signing the petition, stating, "I'd read some Karl Marx during the Depression, which got me thinking about capitalism and how it had brought us into the Depression." Many people thought Marx had the proper concept at the time.'

The file revealed that Capra began work on the Soviet project at Metro-Goldwyn-Mayer in 1932. This was later cancelled because the studio considered the subject, a sympathetic portrayal of the Marxist social experiment, to be Communist propaganda.

Capra and screenwriter Robert Riskin spent three weeks in the Soviet Union in 1937 while on a world tour to promote Lost Horizon. Capra was greeted by Soviet film directors and treated to the spectacular spectacle of the May Day parade. 'I had gotten jaundiced about the capitalistic system--working for Harry Cohn [at Columbia] will do that,' Capra explained. I could see the benefits of the Communist system, but what tainted it was the low level of living borne by the Soviet people. If Stalin had lived in the same poverty, it would have been something to respect since everyone would have been equal.'

On May 16, 1937, an interview with Capra published in the Soviet journal Izvestia, in which he was cited as remarking, "Your country is young and talented." It appears to me that the future of cinema art is unquestionably yours, rather than in America, where the bosses of cinema think solely of profits and not of art.' Capra's trip to the Soviet Union was documented by American Army Intelligence, as was his participation in a picket line in support of the Los Angeles Newspaper Guild strike in 1938. The HUAC file contained an item from the West Coast Communist Party periodical People's World dated 30 May 1938, which indicated that the strike was "Communist inspired," and that Capra was "a member of the picket line."

The file included a report that Capra and Sidney Buchman went to Washington in October 1938 and had visited the FBI at J Edgar Hoover's invitation. Gloria added, 'When Frank Capra went to Washington and spoke with Hoover, it was merely a trick by Hoover to take a look at this film director he and the HUAC were investigating. It didn't help Capra that he expressed some critical things about [President] Roosevelt. Hoover had agents following Capra everywhere.'

As for Sidney Buchman, he had become a Communist in 1938, and his wife, Beatrice, was an influential member of the Hollywood Anti-Nazi League, which was recognized by HUAC as a Communist front group. Capra had addressed the league during a mass assembly in November 1938. Meanwhile, on 14 October 1938 US Army Intelligence had opened its dossier on Capra, and that file had continued to expand until 1947 when it was shown to James Stewart. 'Jim assured them that there was no question about Frank Capra's loyalty to America,' added Gloria.

Jim was nevertheless given the duty of examining Capra. Gloria added that Jim had no intention of investigating his acquaintance, but gave the FBI the idea he would do so. What Jim believed he had to do was convince Capra to prove himself innocent. 'Jim thought he was doing what he had to do,' added Gloria. 'He believed, and I think reasonably, that there was a threat to America and to the film business from the Communists, and he wanted to do something about it. He was Hoover's hidden weapon. He was like an undercover undercover agent.'

No other incident in Hollywood history has caused as much long-term sorrow as the so-called Hollywood witch-hunts. In May 1947, J Parnell Thomas presided over the House Un-American Activities

Committee in Los Angeles. A number of famous Hollywood figures, dubbed 'friendly' witnesses, met with Senator Richard Nixon behind closed doors, handing on names of suspected and known Communists. Actors Robert Taylor and Adolphe Menjou, writers Rupert Hughes and Howard Emmett Rogers, and studio head Jack L Warner were among the 'friendly' witnesses. Stewart was not one of the 'friendly' witnesses, but he was surreptitiously supplying information to HUAC and the FBI.

Those who refused to answer the question, 'Are you now or have you ever been a member of the Communist Party?' were charged with contempt. Those willing to disclose previous membership were asked to name others.

When ten individuals, most of whom were screenwriters, went before the HUAC in Washington in the autumn of 1947, they all asserted the First Amendment. They were later charged with contempt, compelled to return to Washington in 1951 to address the accusation, and eventually imprisoned. A handful of them, like director Edward Dmytryk, agreed to name names in exchange for their release from prison and return to their profession in Hollywood. 'The trouble was, the HUAC didn't perceive Communism to be a political threat,' said Henry Fonda, a Democrat. Because they perceived it as a criminal organisation, the First Amendment had no meaning during those proceedings.'

Many people who were not among the Ten were unable to find jobs because their names appeared on unofficial blacklists and greylists as suspected or known Communists. Those who were Communists, particularly those in the Hollywood Ten who refused to give in, were barred from working in America again (at least until Kirk Douglas violated the blacklist in 1960; as co-producer of Spartacus, he openly credited one of the Ten, Dalton Trumbo). Those who were suspected were placed on the greylist. Some of those people apologised in front of the HUAC and volunteered to name others they suspected of being Communists, so they were allowed to return to work.

Stewart considered the hearings a success because they accomplished their goal of halting the rise of Communism. You may discuss the rights and wrongs of it... and believe me, I haven't always been completely comfortable with what transpired... but you have to put the line in the sand and ask people whether they're willing to cross it. 'And a few of them did.'

Jim was exhausted by the stress of his covert employment. He was continuously debating the rightness and wrongness of his conduct with himself. All he wanted was to drive the thugs out of Hollywood. He also sought to cleanse Hollywood of Communists, but it was secondary to restoring law and order to the streets and the film business. While his efforts to assist the HUAC were clearly appreciated, his efforts to alert the FBI about Mafia activity appeared to be futile.

Chapter 12: Friendships are renewed and destroyed

In 1948, Henry Fonda moved to New York. On Broadway, he starred in Mister Roberts, directed by Joshua Logan, who co-wrote the play with Tom Heggen. The play and Fonda had been a huge success. Fonda toured the play after its lengthy run on Broadway ended in 1952, when he returned to New York for another production, Point of No Return. In 1954, he followed up his successful run with The Caine Mutiny Court Martial.

Fonda had previously avoided Hollywood and movies, but the opportunity to direct Mister Roberts attracted her back to the city. Gloria Stewart couldn't remember what prompted Fonda and Jim's reunion, but it happened sometime in 1954. Her strongest memory is that Fonda simply showed up at their house with a box carrying a model aeroplane kit. There were no words exchanged. Jim merely extended his hand to Hank, who shook it. Then Jim brought Fonda into the house, where they found a spare room, sat down, and began assembling the plane.

'After Jim and I had a disagreement about politics, we didn't communicate for a long period,' Fonda told me. We eventually agreed to disagree but not to discuss politics again.' Gloria claimed Jim assured her that they never agreed they would never discuss politics again. They just knew they wouldn't, and for the rest of their lives, they never said a political word to each other.

When the two buddies were reunited in 1954, they simply picked up where they left off. The only difference was that Hank had remarried; his new wife was Susan Blanchard, Oscar Hammerstein's stepdaughter. Fonda's marriage to Frances had deteriorated as a result of his touring with Mister Roberts, and as the schism increased, Frances suffered from clinical depression. Things didn't get much better when Hank met and fell in love with Susan Blanchard in early 1949. Frances Fonda committed suicide in April 1950. Fonda and Susan married in December 1951.

Jim had a soft spot for Frances, and her death shocked him. Gloria was aware that he disapproved of Fonda's treatment of her, but as the two friends reconcile their differences, Gloria realised that they would never talk about personal values or politics. Jim just refused to pass judgement on Hank, despite his disapproval of Fonda's lifestyle. He cherished his connection with Fonda so much that, having repaired fences, he was not going to sever them again by chiming in with his ideas and opinions regarding Fonda's personal life.

Jim had avoided appearing on television for a long time. 'Back then, you were either a movie or a television actor,' he explained. You couldn't have it both ways. Working on television was regarded as a letdown.' Nonetheless, Jim made his television debut in 1955, in the CBS anthology series G. E. Theatre. He just did it as a courtesy to Ronald Reagan, who hosted the Sunday evening series. NBC had opted to schedule the popular Western series Bonanza at the same time as G. E. Theatre, putting its ratings in jeopardy. Lew Wasserman, Jim and Reagan's agent, urged Jim to appear as a guest on Reagan's show. The result was The Windmill, a thirty-minute Western scripted by Borden Chase in which he played a poor rancher.

In 1957, Jim returned to support Reagan and his TV series with an appearance in Trail to Christmas, a Western adaptation of A Christmas Carol that also marked Jim's directorial debut. But Jim's assistance to Reagan was more than just professional civility. Jim remained engaged in his covert work to bring down the mafia lords who still permeated many parts of Hollywood. The Kefauver investigation into organised crime, which began in 1950, had little impact because J Edgar Hoover was able to redirect public attention away from the proceedings with his apocalyptic warnings about

Communism.

Jim had been keeping tabs on the gangsters who had taken over the rackets since Bugsy Siegel's death. One of these was Mickey Cohen, who rose through the ranks of the Los Angeles Police Department to become one of the city's most powerful mobsters. Cohen was not involved in the film industry, but he was conducting Mafia-sponsored rackets.

Jim never had to speak with anyone from the FBI since Ronald Reagan was his go-between. Hoover thanked Jim for his assistance and encouraged him to continue. Jim believed he was safe as long as he remained anonymous, but Gloria had reason to be concerned. 'Jim wouldn't give up what he saw as a spiritual quest,' she explained. 'I was worried that the hoods would find out what he was up to and take action. We also had our children to consider. But Jim was far too astute. I'm sure he wished he could have led a raid on Mickey Cohen's house like a genuine FBI agent. It was a crime in and of itself that Hoover allowed Jim to act out this charade with no intention of doing anything about it.'

Jim was also responsible for bringing the name of Johnny Rosselli, the official Hollywood liaison and one of Sam Giancana's most trusted lieutenants, to the notice of the FBI. The CIA, on the other hand, was well acquainted with Rosselli. Rosselli served two purposes: while working with the CIA on covert operations, providing Mafia hitmen for the agency's use, he was also in Hollywood looking for failing artists and actresses for the Mafia to "sponsor." Such celebrities would then owe their sponsors. This had long been a hidden aspect of the Hollywood business. Cary Grant and Gary Cooper were early clients, while later clientele included Frank Sinatra and Marilyn Monroe. Giancana and Rosselli are both accused of being implicated in the deaths of Marilyn Monroe and President John F. Kennedy.

Jim knew everything about Rosselli and continued to send information to the FBI through Ronald Reagan.

Jim was invited by President Dwight D Eisenhower to be the primary speaker at the Veterans Day observances at Arlington National Cemetery in Virginia in 1956, both as Deputy Director of Operations for the Strategic Air Command and as a movie star. Jim accepted the invitation with pride.

Following the success of Rear Window, Paramount was eager to have Hitchcock and Stewart collaborate on another project. Jim agreed, and Hitchcock chose to rework The Man Who Knew Too Much, his 1934 thriller. Jim played a doctor on vacation with his wife (Doris Day) and kid (Christopher Olsen) in Marrakesh. He observes a murder and learns about an assassination attempt planned for London. Before he can inform the police, the plotters kidnap his son and threaten him with death if he does not remain silent. As a result, the doctor and his wife pursue the clues to London in order to thwart the conspiracy and save their son.

When The Man Who Knew Too Much premiered in May 1956, the film was a great smash, and Paramount and Hitchcock began planning a sequel, Vertigo. But first and foremost, Jim had a film that he simply had to make. The Spirit of St. Louis, the narrative of Charles Lindbergh's record-breaking flight from Long Island to Paris in 1927, had been given the go light by Warner Brothers. Hayward was experimenting with film production and had signed a three-picture deal with Warners; the first was Mister Roberts, and the third was Hemingway's The Old Man and the Sea.

'Warners, like all the studios at the time in the mid-fifties, were making smaller profits,' Henry Fonda recounted. Then Leland Hayward approached them with his proposal, which Jack Warner believed would provide his studio with much-needed prestige. My sole interest was Mister Roberts, which I felt if anyone was going to do, it should be me because I'd done the part on Broadway for so long.'

When it came to casting Charles Lindbergh, Jim asked Hayward to cast him. 'Warners didn't even want to cast Jim in the role because Jim was twice Lindbergh's age when he made his famous flight,' said Fonda. Lindbergh was twenty-five years old when he took the flight. Stewart was 47 years old. 'I knew they wanted a younger actor, John Kerr, who would have been the proper age,' Joshua Logan recalled. Kerr was little unknown at the time, and his career was brief. He declined to play Lindbergh because he disagreed with his right-wing ideology. Perhaps he made the correct decision for the wrong reasons, because the film's failure could have ruined his career before it began.'

'I was smart enough to know I was twice Lindbergh's age,' Stewart recalled. Hayward worked really hard to get me the part. To begin with, Jack Warner would not hear of it, which I understand. So Warner had Hayward inform me that I didn't get the part, which devastated me greatly. But I was so desperate for the part that I went on a diet to lose the few meagre pounds that middle age had bestowed upon me. I'd never dieted before. Gloria felt concerned when I became so slender. She stated that I appeared unwell. But Warner refused to budge. So I said to Hayward, "Tell Jack Warner I'll dye my hair."

'Jack Warner's desperate urgency to cast the part was what finally got me the part. The studio had spent a significant amount of money on pre-production and hiring Billy Wilder to write the screenplay. Warner was counting the cost and seeing it pile up, and they wanted an actor with some box office muscle, which thankfully I had at the time. So Jack Warner ultimately granted me the part so they could get started since the budget was skyrocketing and they needed to get the results on film.'

Billy Wilder directed the film as well as penned the screenplay. He had concluded that just telling the narrative of the trip would not pique the interest of an audience, so he wrote a screenplay that showed much of Lindbergh's life before the voyage in flashback. 'Billy Wilder wanted to do the picture because Lindbergh was one of his heroes,' Stewart remembered. Leland Hayward wanted to make the film since Lindbergh was a hero of his as well. We all wanted to make the film for the same reasons... and I suppose that's not always the ideal motivation to make a film. Wilder's task was to find a good script. My task was to improve my character. I examined Lindbergh's demeanour. I saw how he walked and listened to how he spoke. I attempted to incorporate some of that into the character, but Wilder always told me, "Don't bury yourself in the part." The general public will have to pay to see Jimmy Stewart." 'I think a lot of Lindbergh's personality was more inside of me than outside of me, but it helped me as an actor.'In the picture, I also did a lot of flying. The studio wouldn't risk allowing me to do too much flying in case I crashed and ruined their film. I was not permitted to fly throughout the filming. 'However, Wilder could obtain close-ups of me taxiing the plane.'I really wanted to fly the plane when they filmed Lindbergh landing in Paris. I wanted to fly the plane, land it, and experience what Lindbergh must have felt when he touched down to the delight of the waiting throng. But they told me I couldn't. Wilder told me, "I admire your dedication and understand your desire."

'I told Wilder, "I think you need to demonstrate your dedication." "What do you suggest?" he asked. "Oh, I dunno... just a little something... like wing walking," I said. He replied, "I'll do it." And he did it. He stood atop the wing of a jet in flight for five minutes.'

Stewart had the opportunity to meet his childhood hero:

'We were filming on Long Island when Lindbergh came to visit. I was overjoyed to finally meet him. I don't think he ever got used to becoming a star... because he was a very quiet, insular type of man.

He didn't have much to say, and there wasn't much time... while I would've liked to chat to him for a long time... but he just had enough time to look at the reconstruction of his original plane we were using, which Lindbergh seemed to like a lot. And he was gone before I could say anything to him. But he did contact me at home one late afternoon... about five... and he had just arrived at the airport and asked Gloria and me what we were doing for dinner. So I informed him we were heading to Chasen's Restaurant, where we always ate, and he responded, "Okay, I'll be there in about twenty-five minutes." So we met him at Chasen's, and he was very pleasant, but he was obviously shy, and it took some time for us to get to know him... but we didn't have long together because Paul Chasen came up to us and apologised, but word had gotten out that Lindbergh was there with James Stewart, and about forty newspapermen and cameramen were waiting outside. So Lindbergh simply asked, "Do you have a backdoor...and would you get me a taxi?" So he thanked us, said goodbye, and departed... and that was the last we saw of him.

'I know Billy Wilder was never satisfied with the entire thing. To begin with, there was never a decent script. Wilder began work on the screenplay and brought in Wendell Mayes to help him make it work. Leland Hayward was also contributing in some way. Wilder recognized that just telling the narrative of the trip would be insufficient, so he included a lot of backstory about Lindbergh's days as a teenage barnstormer. Wilder was at his finest with comedy, and I know he felt this type of film was inappropriate for him--or for him. So he concocted a story about Lindbergh teaching a priest to fly so he could be closer to God! It was simply a little bit of levity.'

Stewart said that Wilder's ingenuity was expressed through the director's conception of a fly that becomes entangled in the plane during flight. 'Wilder couldn't have me flying for so long without saying anything, and he didn't want me--or Lindbergh--just chatting to himself. So Wilder planned that a fly would land on board and

Lindbergh would converse with it to keep himself awake.'

'That was a brilliant idea,' Logan recalled, 'since one of Jimmy's talents as a screen actor is his quirky temperament. And having him converse with a fly was pure whimsy.'

Wilder shot in as many authentic locations as possible, including New York, Nova Scotia, Newfoundland, the Irish coast, across the Channel, and in Paris. His insistence on shooting on location increased the budget from $2 million to $6 million. The picture had barely grossed $2.6 million by the end of 1957. Jack Warner described it as a "disastrous failure."

'Of the three films Leland produced for Warners, Mister Roberts was the only one that fared well,' Fonda recalled. I felt bad for my friend Jim because he was so personally and emotionally invested in The Spirit of St. Louis, and no one came to watch it. I believe Jack Warner liked to blame the film's failure on Jim's age, but I don't believe that was the case. I don't believe the audience perceived Jim as a middle-aged actor attempting to play a young man. They simply liked Jimmy Stewart, and I've never really worked out why they didn't go see him in that movie.'

'It was a dream of mine to play Charles Lindbergh,' Jim says of the film's failure. He was my childhood idol. That photo is hilarious. Some movies, like It's a Wonderful Life, just don't do well when they first come out. In later years, it achieved classic status. But The Spirit of St. Louis was a flop at the time.'

'I think the actual reason the film tanked was not because Jimmy Stewart was too old, but because the film had no fascinating story,' Logan added. Nobody cared that Lindbergh flew in record time from New York to Paris. That wasn't the interesting narrative of Lindbergh, despite Jimmy's belief. The kidnapping and death of Lindbergh's baby [in 1932] would have made for a compelling story.

As for the title, 'The Spirit of St. Louis,' everyone assumed it was a musical. They should have called it The Lindbergh Story, given Jimmy's previous efforts, The Stratton Story and The Glenn Miller Story. Who the hell knew the plane's name was St. Louis?'

The Spirit of St. Louis was Jim's first box office disaster in several years, despite being regarded as a masterpiece today. Even before the film's failure, Jim was entangled in a controversy centred on his status as a pilot and officer in the Air Force Reserve.

The Air Force nominated three Reserve major generals and eight Reserve brigadier generals in February 1957. President Eisenhower had given his approval to the list. James Stewart was one of the candidates for brigadier-general. Maine Senator Margaret Chase Smith, an Air Force Reserve member, began receiving complaints from previous and present Reserve Officers Association administrators that Jim was being treated unfairly just because he was a movie star. Senator Smith studied all eleven submissions and concluded that none of them deserved to be promoted. Her harshest criticism, however, was directed at James Stewart (though she also objected to John Montgomery, a colonel who had retired from the Air Force after many years of service to take an executive position with American Airlines and later with General Electric).

She recalled that Stewart had only served one fifteen-day tour as a reservist since the war's end (in 1956), and had only worn his uniform eight times in peacetime. She also questioned his competence to fly any modern jet aircraft and expressed amazement that he was still the Strategic Air Command's Deputy Director of Operations. She questioned Pentagon officials if they thought James Stewart, who played a key role in Strategic Air Command, deserved to be promoted to brigadier general. They claimed to have done so. 'Then why don't you appoint June Allyson a brigadier-general to portray the female lead in the film?' she replied.

Jim's nomination was defeated by a 13-0 vote in a Senate committee in August 1957. 'I don't think Senator Smith was furious with me personally,' Jim subsequently said of the dispute. I understand why someone would believe that a movie star does not inherently qualify for a high position. But nobody expected me to jump into a modem jet and go off. That was not the plan for me, according to the Air Force Reserve. They had me in line for the position of deputy director of the Office of Information, which I easily handled.'

However, the debate raged on. The Senate's rejection of Jim's promotion was not the end of the story for the Air Force.

Following the failure of The Spirit of St. Louis, Jim believed his next film would be a surefire hit. Night Passage was a Western produced by Aaron Rosenberg at Universal. Borden Chase created the screenplay once more, this time about two brothers, one of whom (played by Stewart) is good and the other (played by Audie Murphy) is an outlaw. The good brother takes on the task of guarding a $10,000 cargo, while the outlaw brother assists in its theft. Finally, the outlaw repents and sacrifices his life to save his brother's during a confrontation with the thieves.

Anthony Mann had been chosen as the film's director. According to producer Rosenberg, he worked on pre-production and shot some of the opening shots. 'But Tony wasn't happy,' Rosenberg explained. 'He didn't like the writing. In comparison to his past Westerns with Jimmy, it just didn't work--and I had to concur. Mann told me shortly after starting work on the picture, "I can't do this." "I'm leaving." "But you'll be disappointing Jim," I added. You're going to let me down." "I put up with Thunder Bay and Strategic Air Command," he explained. I even told Jim The Glenn Miller Story. But I'm not going to manufacture this garbage."

'When Jim heard this, they got into a heated debate. All I know is that Tony accused Jim of only wanting to make a Western in which he could play his damn accordion--and he did play his accordion in the film--and Jim was so offended that he never spoke to Mann again. I anticipated Jim to leave the picture as well. But he refused to leave. For one thing, he admired Audie Murphy because of his distinguished military record. He also enjoyed the concept of portraying a hero in a Western for a change. I think Jim had grown tired of playing the anti-hero, the man filled with hatred and rage that drives him to violence. He even got to sing a couple of songs ["Follow the River" and "You Can't Get Far Without a Railroad"), which Tony Mann also objected to.'

James Neilson, who had worked as a stills photographer before producing television shows and was later hired by Walt Disney to direct several family adventures in the 1960s, was given the directing job by Universal. Neilson was unable to save Night Passage, arguably Stewart's worst Western.

Jim was hurt by his disagreement with Mann. Gloria claimed that he mentally punished himself for his disagreement with the director who had literally saved his career after the war. 'There was something in Jim that just wouldn't let him forgive Mann--which isn't like Jim. I believe Jim felt he was as much to blame for Mann's success as Mann was for his, and that Mann owed him something. He would have preferred to make amends. He couldn't get himself to do it.

'I believe that if Mann, like Hank [Fonda], had simply shown up on the doorstep with a model aeroplane they could build together, everything would have been fine. Neither man, however, made the effort, and they never spoke again.'

Jim's career as a Western star had peaked with Anthony Mann's departure. He'd never again reach the heights of The Man From Laramie. His career was also waning, and there were only a few good films left.

But he had a new passion in his life. He had always wanted to go on hunting safaris in Africa, and he began making regular trips there with Gloria in the 1950s. Gloria, on the other hand, was more interested in animal conservation, and she eventually persuaded Jim to support conservation over hunting. When their daughter Kelly was older, she would develop an interest in the subject as well.

Chapter 13: The Last Beneficial Decade

Jim could have been forgiven for thinking he would never work again. His next picture, John Ford's The Man Who Shot Liberty Valance, was released in 1962. The movie was only made because John Wayne had a contract with Paramount and convinced them to let Ford make it. They agreed as long as the film had a modest budget, was shot in black and white, and spent the majority of its time in the studio.

The film is so devoid of action and external shots, and so heavily reliant on sound stages, that it almost appears to be a filmed play. However, the movie featured an amazing cast, with Jim playing the lawyer who arrives in Shinbone to set up shop, only to be tagged as the man who shot Liberty Valance (played with terrific villainy by Lee Marvin before he became a major screen hero in The Dirty Dozen). Only later does the lawyer discover that the man who shot Valance was a local cattleman (John Wayne).

On the set, Ford played his usual games, berating John Wayne for being a "lousy actor," as he often did. And it was on the set of this picture that Ford instilled fear in Jim and Woody Strode by accusing Jim of being a racist. 'I didn't particularly like Ford's nasty tactics,' Lee Marvin recounted. It's never worked for me. I would have punched Ford in the mouth, and I believe Ford was aware of this, which makes me wonder why he asked me to perform Donovan's Reef again. Maybe he liked me because I was the type of man who would punch him right back. What I didn't understand was how he could be so cruel to Duke [Wayne] and make a joke about Jimmy Stewart. Jimmy was labelled a racist by Ford. Ford was a racist, Jesus. He was sick of English. He considered the IRA to be heroes. But he didn't consider himself to be a racist. In my opinion, it is."Do you have a problem with blacks?" I asked Jimmy flatly. "Why, do you?" he asked. "Of course I do," I replied. We've been kicking the shit out of them for hundreds of years; I'm worried they'll take it out on me." "You know, Lee, you're the first person who understands how I feel," he remarked. I'm not looking forward to thinking about how we've treated them and what they may do if they had the power."

"'If I heard you right, you're worried about us black folk repaying you white folk for all the misery you've caused us," Woody [Strode] stated as he approached us. I responded by saying, "We've got a valid point, don't ya think?" "We might all get along better if you stopped thinking of us as avenging angels and started thinking of us as just people," Strode stated. The problem is that I can see a moment when all hell will break loose between blacks and whites. Maybe we'll get along after that." And I understood his point, but Jimmy countered, "Why do we have to fight about it?" "Didn't the Civil War result in the abolition of black slavery?" "That wasn't freedom," Strode stated. That was tyranny." And I could see where Strode was coming from. But Jimmy just wasn't getting it.

'Man, we talked a lot about racial issues. I believe Jimmy had a problem with black people, but it was a generational issue. My experience was not much better. When it came to Negroes, Jimmy outperformed many of his contemporaries. In fact, one actor, whom I will not name, was waiting for Woody to arrive on set. "Where's the nigger?" he exclaimed. Duke was going to rip this guy's head off, but Jimmy arrived sooner. I had no idea the guy could get that worked up. He grabbed this actor by the shirt, shredding it, and he had to regain control. However, he was simmering-boiling. And he went on to say, "Don't ever use that word around me again, or I might do something our director will regret because he'll have to replace you with an actor who's not all broken up and reshoot a helluva lot of expensive scenes." I liked Jimmy before that occurred, but now I like him much more.'

Jim remembered his work on The Man Who Shot Liberty Valance

fondly. 'I really enjoyed working with Duke. Vera Miles was a lovely lady. And Lee Marvin was a scary guy... you never knew if he was drunk or sober, 'cause he always seemed the same to me-drunk or sober.' He also loved to remember how Ford had won his battle against Jim's typical cowboy hat, which he'd worn in Two Rode Together. 'He won out because in The Man Who Shot Liberty Valance, I didn't wear a cap at all... on his orders,' he explained.

To Jim's relief, the film was a success, but it couldn't compete with the films he had created with Anthony Mann. However, the fact that Jim had starred in a popular Western was enough for producer Bernard Smith and director Henry Hathaway to cast him in the Cinerama Western epic, How the West Was Won, in 1962.

The story was divided into five segments and encompassed two generations of pioneers. Three directors--Hathaway, George Marshall, and John Ford--took on the massive task. Linus Rawlins, a mountain man who gives up his wicked ways to settle down with Carroll Baker, whose parents and half her family were wiped out when their rafts were stuck in rapids, was played by Jim in the first episode. The episode was directed by Henry Hathaway, who Jim hadn't worked with since Call Northside 777. It also starred Karl Malden, Debbie Reynolds, and Walter Brennan.

In the summer of 1962, Jim arrived at the motel in Kentucky where the rest of the cast of the first episode was staying. 'I'd never met Jimmy Stewart, and didn't meet him until the first morning we'd be filming together,' Carroll Baker recounted. I was terrified because he was a legend. I made sure I was up and ready and waiting at the car early so I didn't keep him waiting. 'The first time I saw him, he stole my breath away since he was dressed in his buckskin and looked just like he'd stepped out of the ancient West's pioneer days. I recall him being quite shy, and he didn't say anything while we were taken to the place. And I couldn't come up with anything to say. "Carroll... have you ever played a game called Count the Cows?" he finally said.

'I said "No."

'Then he asked, "Wall, would you like to play . . . Count the Cows?"

'"I don't know how to play it," I admitted. He went on to say, "Well now . . . you just count all the cows on your side of the road, and I count all the cows on my side of the road . . . and when we reach the location, whoever has the most cows wins." So we spent the next hour playing Count the Cows, and by the time we arrived, we were laughing and talking, and we were excellent friends. He just made me feel completely at ease.'

Filming took place at Paducah, on a little island where the Tennessee and Ohio rivers converge. Because the island was plagued with rattlesnakes, Hathaway dispatched men armed with shotguns to exterminate the snakes. However, some snakes managed to evade being killed. 'Carroll and I were doing this love scene, and Henry Hathaway was directing... and I could see, out of the corner of my eye, this fella scurrying around in the background,' Jim remembered. Henry was enraged. He exclaimed, "Cut! "What are you jumping around for?" Then he said, "There's a snake up in that tree." And as I looked up, there was this snake on a limb right above us, just sorta observing us. "I don't care about the snake," Henry added. He's preoccupied with his own affairs. Never move around like that in a shot again." And so we continued with the scenario... and Carroll... she was a little terrified... she said, "I'm not going to look up," and she kinda performed the role extra close to me... which must have satisfied Henry.'

The documentary How the West Was Won was a big success. However, it appeared to be more of a farewell from James Stewart in a strong part, giving a good performance at the age of fifty-four. 'I felt like the best of my work was behind me by that point,' he explained. 'I was pleased with what I did in the film. I wished to accomplish more. When my character appeared as a dead body in the Civil War episode directed by Ford, I responded, "Let me play the body of my own character." But Ford was so unhappy that he said a double who looked nothing like me could play the part.'

According to George Peppard, who played his son throughout the second half of the film, not being able to play his character, even dead, in the Ford-directed sequence disappointed him: 'Jimmy told Ford that it wasn't going to cost the studio any more to do the single shot because we were all on flat fees. An audience soon forgets a character's name, especially in a film with so many characters. Fie correctly stated that when the men bringing Jimmy's body say to the doctor, "This is Linus Rawlins," a simple image of Jimmy laying dead on the surgeon's table would have made all the emotional difference to the spectator. But the actor who played him looked nothing like him. Ford just didn't like it when people had good ideas.

'I had to do a scene where I talk about how my father once told me a story about meeting a grizzly bear. "Pa said, 'Wall... uh... I was going somewhere but the... er... grizzly bear got there first," the discussion went. I hadn't done a scene with Jimmy, but I wanted the audience to believe I was his son and that we'd spent time together. Everyone does a horrible Jimmy Stewart impression, including me, and I figured doing the bear story in his voice would make all the difference. So I told him, "Tell me this story, and help me do it the way you would say it." So he stayed with me and repeated the story several times until I had the rhythm of his speech about as good as I could get it.'Ford yelled at me throughout the shoot, "Who told you to use that stupid voice?" And that's when I said, "I decided because I'm going to make sure the audience remembers this is Jimmy Stewart who played my father." And Jimmy was thankful for it.'

Jim's next film couldn't be more dissimilar to How the West Was

Won. Mr. Hobbs Takes a Vacation was a charming but overlong comedy. Jim was playing a man his own age for the first time in his career, but he appeared to be older than his fifty-four years. He played a banker who takes his wife and small children, as well as his married daughters, their husbands, and all of his grandchildren, on a disastrous vacation to the California coast in a run-down, rambling house. Henry Koster directed the film for 20th Century-Fox, and Maureen O'Hara played his wife. Although not a terrific film, it was successful enough in 1962 to inspire another Jimmy Stewart comedy, Take Her, She's Mine, directed by Henry Koster.

Although set in Paris, the majority of the picture was shot on the Fox backlot for cost considerations. Jim played the father of an activist daughter (Sandra Dee) who causes so much trouble in his life that he ends up in jail, nearly drowns in the Seine, and is accused of distributing pornography.

Jim enjoyed making the Koster comedies because they didn't require him to travel to far-flung and often difficult locations, and he felt at ease playing a man his own age. In 1962, Jim made another appearance on television, this time for John Ford in Flashing Spikes, the story of baseball pitcher Slim Conway.

The following year, Ford asked Jim to make a cameo appearance in Cheyenne Autumn, which had the potential to be a great Western. The film was notable for its sympathetic portrayal of Indians--critics referred to it as "Ford's apology to the Indians"--and it had a truly epic feel to it. However, Ford was not the right director for such a massive undertaking. He was old and grumpy, and his fashion was out of date. He even inserted a pointless comedy sequence that had nothing to do with the plot right in the middle of the movie. This was the scene in which Jim played Wyatt Earp and Arthur Kennedy played Doc Holliday.

Henry Fonda saw this as yet another slap in the face from Ford.

'When we die, My Darling Clementine, Ford didn't even think Jim could play a Western character,' Fonda said. 'It's not sour grapes on my part because I wouldn't have wanted to do that foolish sequence in what was not a good film, but I understood that Ford was casting Jim as Wyatt Earp as if to say to me, "You're not the only Wyatt Earp in town." I know that Jim believed the whole sequence was a mistake, but he won't confess it publicly.'

Fonda was right: Jim chose to look back on the experience as something that was pure fun. 'The thing about Ford was . . . he liked pulling surprises,' he informed me. 'My last picture with him, Cheyenne Autumn, featured this scenario when Arthur Kennedy and myself had to journey out of town in a stagecoach. And Ford wanted . . . I forget why . . . for Arthur and me to look kinda astonished. So he said to us, "Boys, I'm gonna ask the driver to turn the stage around and ride out the other way." And then he walked to the driver and ordered, "Drive straight ahead." Wall . . . when we pulled out we sure were surprised . . . and so was everyone else who had to jump out of the way.'

The film lost money, and Ford's career was all but over. Jim's still had a little life left in it. He made his third and best Henry Koster comedy, Dear Brigitte, in 1965. He played an absent-minded professor who, among other things, helps his young son, played by Billy Mumy, meet film star Brigitte Bardot.

Just as Jim was thinking he would retire gracefully from the screen, he was offered an excellent script written by James Lee Barrett. It told of a family living in Virginia during the Civil War whose widower patriarch is determined to keep his sons out of the war. But the war takes away members of his family, and he can no longer sit idly by. The film was Shenandoah, the first of three films he made with director Andrew V. McLaglen. Universal Studios, who made the film, considered it to be just a minor project, and McLaglen was left alone to make the picture on location in Oregon with no

Universal executives checking on everything and interfering. McLaglen, who had graduated as a director from television, was to become known for taking as many short cuts as possible to get a picture made on time and within budget. But with Shenandoah, he took more time and care, and a lot of that was due to Jim.

Doug McClure, my co-star, told me, "When you had a scene with Jimmy, and I had a few where it was just him and me, he would finish a take, and Andy would exclaim, "That was wonderful." "I think I can do it better," Jimmy would remark, and Andy would say, "But you were perfect," and Jimmy would say, very slowly and gently, "Let me try it again." So we'd re-enact the sequence, and there was always an improvement, but it was so subtle that I didn't see it until I saw it on film.' 'Jimmy would ask for numerous takes, and each time he was consistent with what he'd done before, except that he'd always find a way to improve everything,' McLaglen recounted. For example, if he scratched his ear on take one, he'd scratch it again on each consecutive take. Perhaps it was a tiny detail, but he'd considered the ear scratching as revealing something about the character or what he was thinking, and he'd never fail to perform those little things with each take. But the scene got better and better until, in the end, Jim had gotten and given you everything he could from a scene. He didn't mind being upstaged either, though I believe he saw an actor who could upstage him as a challenge. He went on to say, "I don't care what they do-they can pick their nose or whatever-just so long as it helps the picture." Strother Martin, who steals every scene he's in and every picture he makes, was in one of them. He's the type of actor who is impossible to ignore. He has a wicked sense of humour. Jimmy had this scene, and Strother was doing his usual thing, and Jim realised by the end of the scene that Strother was the centre of attention. "Who did you say that fella was?" Jim asked. I introduced myself as "Strother Martin." He went on to say, "I'd sure like it if you didn't give him anything else to do in this movie or nobody's gonna notice me." He was, I believe, joking. But he didn't have to be concerned. If anything, Jimmy was so strong in that film that most of the other young performers, with the exception of Doug McClure, seemed lost. And the girls [Rosemary Forsyth and Katharine Ross] performed admirably as well.'

Shenandoah gave Jim his best performance of the 1960s, though reviewers missed it at the time, in 1965. 'To me, his performance in Shenandoah was one of the most underestimated performances ever,' said Andrew V. McLaglen. There was a tour de force, and Jimmy didn't get the credit he deserved. 'Universal should have nominated him for an Oscar.'

McLaglen has a large portion of the blame. Despite making several successful pictures in the 1960s, including five with John Wayne, his work lacks elegance. Despite a superb screenplay, his direction of Shenandoah was unimpressive. Although the picture did well and had some wonderful moments, most of which were delivered by Jim, it was never as good as it should have been.

'Shenandoah was fairly pleasant,' Jim replied. Now, I know it was anti-war and all that, but... but when you produce a picture about a sensitive subject and turn it into propaganda... wall, I'm against that, because dramatic quality is what matters. And Shenandoah had a tremendous tragic element to it, thanks largely to Jimmy Barrett's script.'

To Jim's delight and amazement, he was still working steadily, albeit not as much as he used to. This suited him nicely as he grew older. In 1965, he starred in The Flight of the Phoenix alongside Richard Attenborough, Peter Finch, Ian Bannen, Hardy Kruger, Christian Marquand, Ernest Borgnine, George Kennedy, and Dan Duryea. They all played oil-field workers being airlifted across the Sahara, with the exception of Jim and Attenborough. Jim portrayed the pilot, while Attenborough played the alcoholic navigator who leads them a hundred miles off course, causing the jet to crash in the desert. The film, directed by Robert Aldrich, focused on the survivors' tensions, and the audience was made to feel the desert's scorching heat. Conditions for the actors were not as awful as they appeared; the film was shot in Yuma, Arizona.

Robert Aldrich was aware that Jim was anxious when filming began. 'He'd previously worked with European performers, especially British actors, and considered them a little precious,' Aldrich explained. 'He went into the project wary of a heavyweight ensemble dominated by Brits and Europeans.' (Of course, Peter Finch was Australian, but to many Americans, including Aldrich and Jim, he was part of the British contingent.) 'So for the first couple of weeks, he was kind of distant from them,' Aldrich added. The British actors were curious as to what was wrong with him. They hadn't observed that he wasn't spending much time with the American actors. Jimmy didn't just ignore everyone. He simply preferred to be alone. So the British actors resolved to have fun, and they'd make sure Jimmy had fun as well.

'I guess Jimmy assumed the British actors were inebriated since they clowned around a lot, actually doing infantile things at times. Then we'd stage a scene in which they'd all be stone cold sober--which they had been all along. Jimmy had no idea who they were. But, in the end, he became ridiculous with them.'

'I'd heard a lot about some of the European performers and how they'd attempt to grab every shot from us Americans,' Jim explained. That, however, was not the case. In fact, Dick Attenborough, Hardy Kruger, Ian Bannen, and the others were all a little... insane... in the sense that they liked to have fun. They were like children out to have fun... and they did have fun. They were causing a commotion back in Yuma... and I was wondering if their antics would damage the shot. But before I knew it, I was having a wonderful time as well... right alongside them. I'd never really made a scene before... but there I was, having a good time.'

Ian Bannen described the type of shenanigans they engaged in. 'After the jet crashed in the desert, we had numerous dummies stand in--or lie down--for the deceased guys. Dickie, Peter, and I stole the dummies and loaded them into a car. We drove around Yuma with these dummies and flung them out while driving. Onlookers assumed we were throwing actual individuals out of the automobile. We were like children. Jimmy wasn't sure what to make of us at first, but he quickly warmed up to the idea and was soon riding around with us, throwing dummies out of cars. He'd find a fake machine gun, jump out of the car, and pretend to shoot them gangland style. The cops then confronted us, but when they saw it was Jimmy Stewart, they only issued a warning. Peter Finch, who was fairly inebriated at the time, imagined they'd throw us in jail. Finchie delegated to me the burden of keeping him sober as much as I could, and Jimmy took it upon himself to do the same. It was a lot of fun.'

But there was also tragedy. Stuntman Paul Mantz piloted the plane for the dramatic take-off, but due to a weight imbalance, the jet's wing collided with the sand and crashed. Mantz was assassinated.

The Flight of the Phoenix was a critical and popular success when it was released in 1965. However, good screenplays that would fit Jim were becoming increasingly difficult to come by. The Rare Breed is a comedy Western written and directed by Andrew V. McLaglen. Jim played a cowboy who is persuaded to transport a Hereford bull to a rancher for crossbreeding with a longhorn by Maureen O'Hara and her daughter, Juliet Mills.

'Andy gets on with the job,' Jim remarked of working with McLaglen. He doesn't spend hours setting up photographs and then retaking them. That's how I prefer to work.' Unlike on Shenandoah, Jim appears to have been keen to get the filming underway as soon as possible. 'The trouble with Andy is that he wants to do everything in a hurry--as if it's some kind of virtue,' said Ben Johnson, who was in the cast. It's great to do it quickly for television, which is where Andy came from, but if you want to get it right, take your time. Andy is appealing to me. He's a good man and a good friend, but he doesn't always get what he wants. He simply finishes on time and on budget, and the film turns out to be rather unremarkable.'

And that's exactly what The Rare Breed was: ordinary. It doesn't stand up to the classic James Stewart films.

During the 1960s, there was a problem with American cinema. Many of the great directors had passed away, and many of today's directors, such as Andy McLaglen, come from television. So did Vincent McEveety, who made his feature film debut in 1968 in Firecreek, a James Stewart Western. The two-year gap between The Rare Breed and Firecreek indicates how difficult it had become for Jim to find the perfect vehicle for him. At the very least, Firecreek was unique in that it included Jim and Henry Fonda for the first time since On Our Merry Way twenty years before.

For a change, Fonda portrayed the villain, leading his gang to Firecreek. Jim played a farmer who uses logic and comedy to try to solve the town's problems. Inevitably, the film ends with Fonda attempting to murder Stewart. But Fonda is shot and killed by a lady he has been having an affair with (Inger Stevens).

'He may have been new to the movies, but he did something few directors have been able to do in recent years,' Fonda said of McEveety. He really pushed Jim, and he delivered a fantastic performance. Jim had grown accustomed to presenting the same show around that time, but McEveety wouldn't allow him to get away with it. Jim gives one of his best performances. I thought I did well as well. It's a shame that the studio [Warner Brothers] didn't know what to do with it and just put it into theatres unannounced, and nobody went to see it.'

While Firecreek was in development, Andrew McLaglen was hard at work on Bandolero! 'The film was a package that Darryl Zanuck at Fox dreamed up,' said screenwriter James Lee Barrett. He had a plot idea involving two outlaw brothers. One brother is about to be executed; the other impersonates the hangman and frees his sibling. They abduct a female and cross into Mexico, where they are all slaughtered by bandidos. Zanuck told Andy McLaglen that he wanted him to make the film, and that he wanted Dean Martin and Jimmy Stewart to play the brothers, with Raquel Welch as the kidnapped widow.I believe we came up with a good first part of the story, in which Jimmy rides into town as the hangman and saves Dean from the rope. It was all pretty lighthearted. After they escaped, things became more serious, and it was tough to turn Jimmy Stewart into an outlaw. You simply didn't believe it. So I had to be on set, creating hilarious or characteristic Jimmy Stewart lines, to make it work.'

It was Jim's last successful decade in terms of filmmaking, with most, if not all, of his films ranging from adequate to extremely good. In his personal life, it was a period of tremendous sadness.

Jim left the Air Force Reserve in 1968. Gloria's boys, Ronald and Michael, had already left the house. Michael had ended up in Mercersburg. Ronald, who insisted he didn't enjoy schools in the east, persuaded his parents to let him attend school in Rome since it was close to Jim's ranch in Winecup, Nevada. Ronald attended Colorado State University, where he majored in business studies. Michael studied political science at Claremont College in California. Jim wanted his boys to go to Princeton, but he didn't want to force them into it the way Alex had.

The two boys were maturing into completely different individuals. Michael grew his hair long and criticised right-wing ideologies, particularly the Vietnam War. Ronald was more conservative in nature than his stepfather. When his conscription notice arrived, he regarded it as his responsibility to join the Marines. He had no choice but to be transferred to Vietnam.

Jim, like many other old-school Republicans, was amused by the numerous university rallies against the Vietnam War, expressing his displeasure with anyone who avoided the draft. 'Our country was at war, and when your country is at war, you can't refuse to serve your country,' he explained. Ronald, Gloria argued, did not enlist solely to appease his stepfather. 'Ronald did the right thing, and we were proud of him. We didn't love Michael any less because he had his opinions. Some have speculated that Jim pushed Ronald into enrolling. But that is not the case. Ronald did what he thought was proper.'

Jim had supported the Vietnam War and had visited Southeast Asia on several occasions. During one deployment, he even attended a bombing mission near the Cambodian border. Gloria accompanied Jim on a USO trip to Vietnam in early 1969, where he shook hands with thousands of soldiers and collected notes to present when he returned home. They even got to see Ronald, and Jim snapped a snapshot of Gloria with their son, who was now a lieutenant.

Jim began to work on the comedic Western The Cheyenne Social Club shortly after returning to America. It began as a joy to make since Jim was collaborating with Henry Fonda again, and this time they were portraying buddies. Jim portrayed a cattleman who unexpectedly inherits what he believes to be a tavern called the Cheyenne Social Club. He journeys from Texas to Wyoming to claim his inheritance, only to discover that it is a brothel. Fonda, his dear friend with nothing better to do, joins him.

It was a strangely calm, delightful comedy Western directed by Gene Kelly (yes, the Gene Kelly of all those MGM musicals) and written by James Lee Barrett. It's still entertaining to watch, if only to see Stewart and Fonda in action. They had some great banter, and the opening titles are backed by Jim singing a tune while Fonda tells story after story. It was another solid premise with a good screenplay, but something wasn't working. 'I suppose the only fault with the picture was the choice of Gene Kelly to direct it,' Barrett thought. Not every director can make a Western, but some can produce fantastic musicals. John Ford and Anthony Mann couldn't make a good musical, but they could make a spectacular Western. And if Gene Kelly couldn't turn Hello Dolly! into a brilliant musical, what can he accomplish with a Western?'With stars like James Stewart and Henry Fonda, you'd think it would be difficult for a director to make a bad Western. I wouldn't say it was a bad film because I believe it had some redeeming qualities. But as a Western, it was really bad. Even with those stars, they knew they were in big trouble. Fonda was concerned about the writing, which was handled by my department. Normally, Fonda would have gone to the director and told him about his problems, and the director would have responded, "Leave it with me," and the writer would have sorted it out. But Fonda didn't believe Kelly, so he complained to Jimmy Stewart, who came to me. Fonda's issue was that he believed his role was overshadowed by Stewart's. Jimmy explained it to me this way: "Hank hasn't got enough to say."So I reworked the entire opening sequence--which was basically just for the credits to roll--in which Stewart and Fonda ride for a hundred miles or so, with Fonda chatting the entire time. "Do you realise you've been talking all the way from Texas?" Stewart finally asks. and Fonda responds, "I was just trying to keep you company."And Fonda loved that, so we incorporated it into the film, where he says a lot at first and makes Jimmy so upset that he doesn't say anything else for the rest of the film.'

The issues on the set paled in comparison to Jim's biggest nightmare: Ronald was murdered while commanding a five-man patrol in Quang

Tri on June 11, 1969. Gloria remembered being at home on North Roxbury Drive that evening. Kelly and Judy were getting ready for their Westlake graduating prom when she noticed a military contingent approaching her front door--at that moment, she knew Ronald had been slain.

Jim returned home immediately, and a memorial service was planned. A representative from the Pentagon arrived a few days after Ronald's death to discuss plans to publicise Ronald as a hero in order to supply propaganda for President Nixon. Jim's rage nearly erupted, but he kept it under control, seizing the guy by the arm and screaming through gritted teeth, 'Let me take you to the door now.' 'I thought he was going to punch the fella out,' Gloria said, 'but he controlled his temper, which is all to his credit.'

Gloria admitted she was a "total wreck" after Ronald died. 'Every night for weeks, I just wept myself to sleep.' She added that it was a difficult period since Jim didn't allow himself to grieve, which she believed stopped her from grieving her loss. 'It wasn't because Ronald was my son rather than his,' she explained. 'Ronald, like Michael, was as much Jim's kid as anyone.' Jim seemed to be unable to express his true feelings.

'I could see that Gloria wanted to grieve, but Jim just never showed those types of feelings, even if he was breaking up inside,' Fonda said. What was so heartbreaking was Gloria's perception that Jim did not allow her to grieve. The trouble is, he was doing his best to cope with the loss, and it got in the way of Gloria's needs. That's what occurs when people you care about pass away. You have a strange tendency to blame others--mostly each other. They resented their other son, Michael, in some ways because they thought he had abandoned the family--but he hadn't. He simply did not believe in the war, and he did not believe his brother's death was worthwhile.'

Ronald was posthumously awarded the Silver Star in September

1969. Jim and Gloria attended the award ceremony, which was held at the Marine base in El Toro, California.

Jim returned to work on The Cheyenne Social Club much before he should have. But, while he didn't look to be in mourning, he was undoubtedly battling to keep himself from sinking into despair. 'Ronald's death just tore Jimmy apart, and he lost all interest in the picture,' Barrett recounted. It's to his credit that it doesn't show in his performance, but he didn't have the courage to confront Gene Kelly about Kelly's faults, and Fonda was clearly more concerned about his friend than he was about the film. That picture could have been a good Western with the appropriate director, say, Henry Hathaway. "Don't dwell on your loss," Hathaway would have yelled at Jimmy. "Pay attention to the damn movie." He would have sounded like a bully, but he would have done it all for Jimmy's sake.

'Kelly felt he was helping Jimmy by shooting around him anytime he noticed Jimmy was down, or he'd just cancel the day's work, which I don't think helped anyone. Gene's heart was precisely where it should be. But, to be honest, they needed Henry Hathaway to push Jimmy, or Kelly should have cancelled all future production until Jim was ready. To be fair to Kelly, I'm sure he simply didn't know what to do. And he's a really kind guy. But his worst error was not admitting that he had no idea how to construct a Western in the first place.' 'When Jimmy told me about Ronald, I saw my friend looking older and wiser than ever,' Fonda recalled in 1976. He'd aged during the [Second World] War, and he aged again when that dreadful news arrived. When something like that happens, you just don't know what to say. I attempted to cheer him up with yams about the "good ol' days" until I realised how silly it all sounded in comparison to what he was going through. I was like, "Sorry, Jim, I'll just keep my mouth shut." "No, Hank, just keep talking," he said. You know... when you were talking about Duke [John Wayne] wrapping a boa constrictor around your head while you were sleeping in that bar in Mexico... it reminded me of the time you and I were back in New York, and we found a rat in our apartment, and it turned out it was living in your shoe... and you put that shoe on, and that rat shot out, more terrified than you were." And he started laughing, and we just kept reminiscing, which helped Jim block out the misery for a little time.'"Hank, if you see me getting low, just tell me a story," he urged. It is quite beneficial." That's exactly what I did. But I had the impression that his attempts to bring himself out of depression were more for my benefit than his, because he could see how hard I was trying to keep my spirits up while he was struggling to keep his up. As if I were the one in need of assistance. And Jimmy Stewart is the kind of friend I have. The best of all possible worlds. When he is in pain, he thinks of you.'

Another tragic episode occurred when Jim's favourite horse, Pie, proved too old to endure the filming. 'That horse had to be twenty-seven... twenty-eight years old... which is getting on for a horse,' Jim said. The last photograph I took of him, The Cheyenne Social Club, was taken in Santa Fe, New Mexico, at an elevation of over 6,000 feet... and it was too much for ol' Pie. I couldn't put him to use... I had to utilise his backup. He died not long after that.'

'Jimmy adored ol' Pie,' Fonda said. And when Pie found it too difficult to work at that height, Jimmy suggested, "Let Pie rest." "I need another horse." I decided to surprise Jimmy by sneaking up to Pee with my sketchpad and sketching Pie whenever Jimmy wasn't looking. After the film was over, I painted Pie and gave it to Jimmy. It meant even more to him since Pie died two weeks after we finished the film; Jimmy had lost his stepson and now his horse, and it was just too much for him.'

'Hank is a fantastic artist, and his portrait of Pie is really gorgeous,' Stewart recalled. Hank has captured his personality perfectly. I hung the image in my library, where it will remain forever. In some ways, it gives me the impression that Pie is still with me. I believe there is a place where we go after we die. It's heartbreaking to lose someone in this life, but they'll be waiting for us after we die. Pie will be there to greet me. Meanwhile, I keep some of his soul with me... in that painting of Hank's... hanging in my library.'

National General, a short-lived company that made a few films and then failed to properly distribute them, produced and released The Cheyenne Social Club. As a result, the film, which is actually a simple and entertaining watch, tanked in 1970. (In the UK, the releasing arm of the Cinerama production company--where I worked--inherited all of the company's pictures, but it was too late to save any of them from disaster.)

Life had to carry on for the Stewart family after Ronald died. Judy and Kelly, the twin girls, went their separate ways after graduating from Westlake, though both had developed an interest in different cultures after travelling to locations like Africa with their parents. Judy worked as a jungle guide in Nepal before moving to Tanzania to work on a coffee farm. When a cholera outbreak occurred, she returned to California and married, becoming Judy Merrill.

Kelly graduated from Stanford with a BA in anthropology and a PhD in zoology from the University of Cambridge in England, where she met her future spouse. She then travelled to Rwanda and Kenya to research gorillas.

Michael married three weeks after his brother died. He found himself at odds with his mother and stepfather, who he believed felt he had been unsupportive of their views on Vietnam.

Back on North Roxbury Drive, Ronald's death appeared to reverberate through every room in the Stewart home. Gloria explained, "We were just getting on each other's nerves." Jim sought to avoid Gloria's attention by playing golf with Fred MacMurray at the Bel Air Club every morning. On weekends, he flew his Super

Piper Cub plane. 'He just seemed to be in a state of shock-like he was in a trance and wouldn't allow anyone pass an invisible barrier,' Gloria added. That was his method of expressing his grief. I was still prone to breaking down. I started to worry about our marriage. But, I suppose, many people go through similar difficulties after a bereavement. But losing a kid is something no parent should have to go through. That's not how it's intended to be. We felt as if we had lost both boys in some ways, because Ronald was gone and Michael was studying law and staying away from us. It had been the worst of times.'

Gloria's situation was really worse than Jim's; within fifteen months of losing Ronald, she also lost her mother, sister, and brother. She only survived because of her incredible resilience and commitment to live each day to the fullest for the rest of her life.

Chapter 14: The Television Years

While Gloria was battling with her insurmountable challenges, Jim was offered a lifeline by a desperate New York producer, T Edward Hambleton. Financial difficulties threatened to close Hambleton's Phoenix Theatre, so the producer devised a plan to restore Mary Chase's play Harvey. When Hambleton learned that James Stewart would love to reprise his role as Elwood P Dowd, he made Jim an offer.

'I thought it was a great concept,' Jim replied. 'I figured I was finally at the perfect age to play Elwood. Actually, I'd considered recreating the play myself several times over the years... but film commitments had always kept me from doing so. Or maybe I was just too afraid to take the risk.'

Surprisingly, he did not immediately accept Hambleton's offer. 'When Jimmy realised that we would be trying out the play first before the students of the University of Michigan, he backed away,' Helen Hayes, who had consented to be in the play (as a Phoenix Board member), informed me. "None of those kids have probably heard of me," he explained. And if they have, they probably only know me as someone who did not protest the Vietnam War, and they will despise me." So I told him, "The kids who protest are only against war, not you." And if they don't know who you are, they certainly won't know who I am, so we'll keep each other company." That put an end to his dithering. So we did the play [in February 1970], Gloria came out to be with Jimmy, and they were put up in the best hotel, but they didn't like the food there, so they started eating at the university restaurant. To his amazement and delight, all these students continued approaching him in the restaurant and asking for his autograph since, of course, they knew who James Stewart was. Someone thought he was being harassed by these pupils and proposed they be barred from approaching him. He went on to state, "When they don't come up to me . . . that's when I'll start worrying."'

Jim stated that reenacting the play made him realise that 'you can't represent Elwood as a crazy man. The trick is to persuade the audience that this large white bunny is truly your friend. You have to make the viewers wish they had their own huge white rabbit pal.' He also believed that America needed 'another dose of Elwood P Dowd' at a time when it was divided by the Vietnam War.

Jim received wonderful reviews when the play was relocated to the Phoenix Theatre in New York. 'He's a genuine star, with the presence, projection, audience sense, and personal charm to command a theatre,' stated Variety. He gives the sense of not performing at all.' The New York Daily stated, 'Stewart gives a master class in acting with each performance.' 'His garrulous, cheerful presence is a treat,' noted the New York Times. 'You have the impression that, apart from Harvey himself, there is no one you would prefer to meet in your favourite neighbourhood pub [than Stewart].' (I can speak to this having spent countless dinners with Jim and Gloria.)

Harvey was to usher Jim into a new chapter of his career, returning him to the stage where he began, even as his film career was coming to an end. In fact, Jim's career would only include one more prominent role in a major picture. Jim, Strother Martin, and a teenage Kurt Russell starred in Andrew V. McLaglen's Fool's Parade (also known as Dynamite Man From Glory Jail). However, a corrupt officer (George Kennedy) and a corrupt bank president (David Huddleston) are determined to obtain the $25,000 that Jim has earned in prison and with which he and his friends hope to build a business. McLaglen recalls, "When I first talked to Jimmy about the project, and I told him he'd have Strother Martin as his co-star, Jimmy responded, "Who's Strother Martin?" "You had a scene with him in Shenandoah," I explained. "You said he stole the show." He wiped his chin and answered, "Yeah... I think I remember him." Wall... you'd better let me think about it." And he spent the next four days debating whether he wanted to make an entire film with Strother Martin. People think of Jim as slow because he takes his time and thinks things out. But he's incredibly sharp. Finally, he added, "Tell Strother Martin he's got the part." Jim was well aware that he'd struggle to avoid being overshadowed by Strother, but I believe he saw it as a challenge.

'Jim, on the other hand, knew when to draw the line. One day, he looked over the call sheet and noticed that Strother was supposed to be holding a pencil, a pad, and a bit of string. "Look, Andy, you got Strother with a pencil, and that's all right," Jimmy said to me. He also has a pad, which I can cope with. But there's no way you're going to get me in front of a camera with that guy and a piece of string." So we removed the string. It may not appear to be much, but Jimmy knew that Strother Martin playing with a bit of string would steal the show. But Jimmy adored Strother. They had a great time together.'

Fool's Parade, released in 1971, suffered from McLaglen's poor directing once more, and it passed fast. Jim couldn't have realised it at the time, but his career--aside from a few cameos--had practically followed the same path as the film.

There were now no movie offers, or none that Jim believed were worth considering, so he considered a novel idea-a regular TV show. He'd actually been appearing on Jack Benny's annual performance for numerous years. Benny, one of the Stewarts' neighbours and a personal friend, had persuaded Jim and Gloria to appear on his once-a-year show, in which they portray a Hollywood star and his wife who are constantly plotting to flee the comedian's miserly ways but always wind up in his unwanted company. Their appearances on his show persuaded NBC that a situation comedy starring Jim could be successful. As a result, The Jimmy Stewart Show was a smash hit in 1971. Jim would play a professor who is having troubles at work and at home.

The show needed a starring lady, and Jim immediately suggested Gloria. NBC had no plans to consider Mrs Stewart since they wanted Julie Adams. Hal Kanter, the show's producer, had the unfortunate responsibility of breaking the news. He cleverly recommended to Jim that he think about whether he wanted to get up every morning with Gloria, spend long days on a soundstage with Gloria, and then go home with Gloria every day for at least twelve weeks. 'That made a lot of sense to me,' Jim remarked. 'That was a certain way to end a marriage. I didn't realise NBC had already decided they didn't want Gloria at the time, or I would have told them what they could do with their program.'

The Jimmy Stewart Show was shot for two seasons, 1971 and 1972. Gloria was well aware that Jim had rapidly developed a dislike for it. Each thirty-minute episode took four days to rehearse and two days to film. 'That was too fast for Jim, but that's how television worked,' she recalled. 'As an actor, he was disappointed. Everyone enjoyed watching him be himself, but he didn't want to be himself. That was the show's strength, but it was also Jim's weakness. He desired something to test him. I advised him to relax and enjoy being himself, but I think the show's speed finally got to him.'

Jim's long-time buddy Leland Hayward died during the first season's production in 1971. Jim fell into a deep depression, but he managed to pull himself out of it.

Then something happened that Woody Strode thought confirmed Jim's racism. 'A black actor named Hal Williams had been cast as an FBI agent in one episode, but Jimmy Stewart got confused with another episode in which a cop was intended to play Jimmy's character,' Strode explained. He mistook Hal for the cop who was having a go at him, so he called for the producer and ranted about how blacks were pushing white people around all over the country, and now they had this black cop pushing him around, and he wasn't having any of it. It was pointed out to him that Hal wasn't portraying the white cop, but rather an FBI agent in another episode.'

'I wasn't ripping out black folks,' Jim responded when I asked him about the episode. I was chiding the idea that there were all these black Americans moaning all across the country and bossing politicians about, as if nothing else mattered.' 'We don't talk about black people,' Gloria told me away from Jim's ears. Jim is concerned about racism and civil rights.'

Director Peter Bogdanovich wanted Stewart to co-star in The Last Picture Show in 1971, but his commitment to the TV series prevented him from doing so. So Ben Johnson got the part, and he won an Oscar for it. Despite this, Bogdanovich had another plan for Jim, as well as John Wayne and Henry Fonda. 'There was this concept that Peter Bogdanovich had to film a Western with Duke, Hank, and me,' Jim recounted. He admired the works of Henry Ford and [Howard] Hawks. He first told me about it while bringing me to lunch. And he told me about his plan. There was no script, only an idea. It was more of a "If we did it, we could do this and that." I loved his ideas and instructed him to get a script so we could go over them more. You can't accomplish anything unless you have a script. So he went away and returned a few weeks later with a script. I was dissatisfied. There wasn't much of a story, and the jokes were mostly about how elderly we were all, and I felt like you could make the joke once and it would be hilarious, but to make an entire film about it... wall, I felt like we were somewhat lampooned. So I contacted Duke and asked if he'd seen the screenplay, which he had, and he said, "Jimmy boy"--I liked it when he called me Jimmy boy because he's younger than me--"Jimmy boy, they're trying to make three old fogies out of us." I agreed, and Hank agreed, and that was the end of it. But we were all disappointed because we all wanted to make a movie together... all three of us. We'd never all been in a photo together before. And Bogdanovich was let down. We could have done anything if he had written a better script.'

Jim's sorrow was compounded when his sister Virginia died of a strangulated hernia in April 1972. Jim always kept his tears to himself at funerals, and when he saw Virginia's bereaved husband Alexis crying, he urged him, "Don't cry in front of all these people." If you must cry, do so alone.' 'Jim was quite angry with Alexis,' Gloria said to me. 'I thought Jim was wrong, but I got it.'

The Jimmy Stewart Show disbanded after only two seasons. 'They gave me too much authority,' Jim said, blaming himself for the show's failure. I had screenplay and casting permission. I had the last say over everything, as if I were the producer... and the problem is, I'm just an actor. I had no authority to make any of those decisions. I made some poor decisions.'

There was still some work to be done. Jim narrated Pat Nixon: Portrait of a First Lady, a documentary on President Richard Nixon's wife, in 1972. He decided to take the job because he was a staunch Republican.

J Edgar Hoover died in 1972, as well. For some time, reports about the FBI director's homosexuality had been floating, and within a few years of his death, stories about the many secret papers he'd saved and ordered burned when he died began to circulate. One of those files concerned Jim and Henry Fonda. Fonda was particularly vehement about Hoover's secret files when he spoke about them in 1976: 'Hoover investigated anyone who was rumoured to be engaged in what might be dubbed "immoral acts," which ranged from criminal activity to promiscuity and homosexuality.'I don't think there was a single Hollywood star from the 1930s to the 1950s who didn't have some sort of FBI file on them. Jim adored and liked J Edgar Hoover, even if I disliked him. So it didn't hurt me as much as it did Jim, who had long considered Hoover to be one of our country's greatest heroes. They were even close. However, Jim was able to forgive Hoover because he believed he understood Hoover's motivations. That's Jim's Republican side. But it was clear to me that Hoover was the worst thing that had ever happened to law and order in America.'

Throughout the 1980s, Jim became increasingly resentful of Hoover. 'It really wounded Jim to believe that J Edgar Hoover, for whom he'd done all those secret things, had a dossier on him and Hank Fonda,' Gloria said. Jim used to talk a lot about Hoover. We no longer mention his name.'

Jim agreed to a new film version of Harvey from Hallmark Television in 1972. He thought it was better as a stage play than a film, although it was an improvement over the original cinema version. 'When I performed Mister Roberts on stage all those years and then did the film version, the movie failed to capture something that was the core of the play,' Jim explained. That is why plays are plays and films are films, and a film adaptation of a play will never be as good as the play, just as a film will never work as well as a play. So I understand Jim's statement that Harvey is a better play than a film. But believe me when I say that no one can play Harvey better than Jim on stage or in film.'

Jim was persuaded to reprise his role as a lawyer in Hawkins on Murder, a full-length CBS television movie. The character earned him a Best Actor award from the Hollywood Foreign Press Club, and the popularity of the first Hawking film led to seven more.

'I enjoyed that Hawkins series,' Jim said of Hawkins. 'I did them because I'd always wanted to play a lawyer since Anatomy of a Murder,' she says. I was a defence lawyer, and I enjoyed how my character acted in the trial lawyer game. He argued the law when the facts were against him. When the law was on his side, he argued the facts. When the facts and the law were both against him, he slammed his hands on the table.'

Strother Martin, his scene-stealing co-star from Shenandoah and Fool's Parade, was his regular co-star in Hawkins. Jim had no problems with Martin because he might well need someone to help shoulder the load... as I'm not getting any younger'. 'I don't care what Strother does... just don't let him carry a piece of string,' he added.

'I created eight of those pictures for television... in just two years... but in the end I had to give it up,' Jim says of Hawkins. It was all a little bit frantic for me. I'd been in films that were rushed, but they were never shot as quickly as television. I simply couldn't keep up. I had so many lines to learn and so little time, and when you're no longer a young man, you don't remember lines as easily as you used to. "I can't do this," I stated once. "I'm having trouble remembering my lines." "You know, Jim, it's okay for you to use cue cards," the director stated. "Many actors do." I went on to say, "But I can't see the cue cards."'

Another loss occurred in 1973, when one of his closest friends from his MGM days, Bill Grady, died. Then, while working on one of Hawkins' pictures, John Ford died. Jim returned to work after attending the funeral. But he was unusually irritable, and after exploding over something inconsequential, he abruptly paused and questioned, 'What am I doing?' 'He felt lost,' Gloria explained. His friends were all dying. "I'm losing all my old friends, and I'm not making any new ones," he frequently told me. (According to Gloria, Jim gladly accepted me as a welcome guest at their hotel whenever they visited England.)

On a lighter note, Jim and Gloria reconciled with Michael, who gave Jim and Gloria their first grandchild in 1973. 'A grandchild can do a lot to repair a family's scars,' Gloria added.

MGM released That's Entertainment in 1974, a fantastic compilation film looking back on their many musicals. Jim was one of the show's main narrators. That same year, he lost another pal, Jack Benny. Jim went through a period of depression after each death, but he always got back up. 'It's amazing how he finds strength,' Gloria said to me in the early 1980s. 'He'll tell you that his strength comes from God, but I believe it comes from the guy himself.'

As if to shake off the cobwebs of melancholy, Jim chose to stage Harvey in London in 1975, and it was at the Prince of Wales Theatre that I first met him. 'Sir Bernard Delfont suggested I come and do the play,' Jim explained. (Because I had worked with Sir Bernard, we were able to chat about him briefly. Because Jim was a famous star and I was only a member of staff, our experiences were radically different!) Jim had pretty much concluded that his film career was done. 'I don't think I'll be making any more movies,' he remarked. I simply do not fit in. Some of the scripts that are still given to me confuse me. I don't seem to fit in with today's cinema. Producers and directors have no idea what to do with me, and I have no idea what to do in their films. Everything is quite aggressive. Films appear to be cruel. They're downright depressing. They are cynical.'All of these Clint Eastwood flicks make no sense to me. I don't. . . I'm not sure why Fonda felt compelled to film one of those spaghetti Westerns [Once Upon a Time in the West]. They're the movies that ruined the Western with their brutality and... and... and... cynicism.'

'But, Jim, it was the films you made with Anthony Mann that contained those very elements,' I pointed out. Those films forever altered the Western genre. Today's successful Westerns are a direct result of the pictures you and Anthony Mann created. You influenced Clint Eastwood. Anthony Mann influenced today's few good Western directors.'

That made him sit back in silence, as if he had never thought about it. 'Then I guess I'm just getting too damn old,' he finally muttered. It's just that... all the screenplays I read--and there aren't many these days--have some grumpy old grandfather in them, and I say to myself, "Golly, I wonder who they're thinking of getting for that part," and then I realise it's me. I don't want to be a miserable grandfather. I'd like to try something a little more interesting. But they no longer compose parts like that.

'I have to make room for the new fellas... like Eastwood, Redford, and Newman,' he says. I'm not bothered. My life has been fantastic... a good life. Right now, I'm just having fun playing Harvey. 'I have no idea what the coming year will bring.'

As it turned out, Jim returned to the big screen the next year. He appeared as the doctor who confirms the aged gunfighter's ailment as cancer in the final John Wayne film (and one of the Duke's greatest), The Shootist. 'Our first scene, an interior, was the doctor's office, and there I met James Stewart, who was worried about his old friend, Duke,' said Don Siegel, who directed The Shootist. Jimmy was a hoot. He went on to say, "Are you shooting the left side of my face?" "Yes," I said. Is there something wrong with that? "Do you have a stronger side?" "Nope," Jimmy responded with a smile. "My best side is whichever side the camera is pointing at."

'Then Duke appeared on the set, and he and Jimmy hugged. "Gentlemen, this scene is very touching," I said. However, I hope you agree that we should play against that. All the sorrow, agony, and pathos will be there if you play the situation matter-of-factly and don't allow sentimentality to come in." "Don't you hate it when the director's right?" Duke asked Jimmy. And Jimmy stated, "I just hate it."They performed flawlessly in their scenes. The only difficulty was that Jimmy was deaf, so I had to shout directions at him. "What are you shouting for?" Jimmy said. Duke simply laughed.'

That same year, Jim appeared in Airport '77 (so-called since it was released in 1977). The billionaire owner of a luxury jet that is hijacked and subsequently crashes into the ocean appears briefly and is largely seen at home waiting for word of the heroic rescue attempts.

With little employment on the horizon, Jim was kept busy by Gloria's energy and sense of adventure. By the mid-1970s, he was frequently visiting Rwanda to advocate gorilla conservation, accompanied by Gloria and daughter Kelly. He braved his nearly seventy years by clambering around at a height of 11,000 feet, photographing gorillas. 'They're terrifying monsters,' he said. My daughter Kelly says that if I don't represent a threat, they won't hurt me. But there was this one guy--huge and hairy--who was only six feet away from me. He was simply staring at me... and I was kind of staring back. I grabbed my camera and focused; it's a good thing the film was quick because I was trembling so badly.'

Gloria kept him more active than ever before, travelling abroad and attending social functions-'anything to keep him moving and feeling alive,' Gloria recalled. 'I know people think I push him too hard, but you can't let ageing stop you, or you'll stop for good. As a result, I keep Jim going. And he enjoys it when he begins to tell one of his stories. He has the ability to make a good narrative last a long time. Lots of pauses and word-drawing. He'll have a room full of people listening to him, and he'll be fantastic every time. 'Doesn't always convey the truth, but his stories are fantastic.'Such as the one about Pie. He recalls a moment in which the horse was forced to travel down the street by himself, and on his saddle is a small bell that tinkles as he walks. The camera had to keep up with the horse. Anthony Mann went on to say, "How are we gonna get the horse to walk on cue and keep going until I've got the shot?" As a result, Jim tells him, "Leave the horse to me." "When you hear the director say 'Action!' you start walking down the street... and you don't stop until you hear him holler 'Cut!'" Jim says to Pie. "Do you have that?" And Jim adds to the story each time he tells it. As a result, when Mann yells "Action!" the horse begins to walk and continues until he hears

"Cut!"

'I'm not sure how factual that story is, but it grows taller every time he repeats it. Jim has a priceless gift of making others happy.'

Chapter 15: Honoured until the end

In 1976, Jim kept himself busy by campaigning in California for Ronald Reagan in the presidential primaries. He also narrated Sentimental Journey, a documentary commemorating the 50th anniversary of the DC-3, an early civil aircraft built for the US Army Air Force. Jim had, in fact, narrated a number of documentaries over the years, usually about subjects or causes in which he was personally invested. Thunderbolt, a 1947 documentary directed by William Wyler about fighter-plane support of ground troops during WWII, and How Much Do You Owe?, made in 1949 to benefit the Disabled American Veterans, were among them.

When Jim's other sister, Dotie, died of cancer in 1977, Gloria kept up the pace. She knew Jim didn't want to lose himself in his grief, so she gave him little time to mourn. 'But there are times when he goes off in his mind to some place even I can't reach,' she explained. I believe he's reflecting on his life, remembering friends and family who have died. I'd hear him say quietly, "It won't be long before I'm with you all." But he doesn't say it in a mournful tone. He's very... wistful about it. Almost with a smile. He believes in God and heaven, and he believes they are all waiting for him.' 'I'm not taking a chance on something better after death,' Gloria said. 'I'm making the most of this life.'

Jim and Gloria travelled to London in 1977 to attend the wedding of their daughter Kelly to University of Cambridge lecturer Alexander Harcourt. That same year, Jim returned to England to make a cameo appearance in Michael Winner's terrible remake of The Big Sleep. Jim appeared in only two scenes, playing another millionaire who hires private investigator Philip Marlowe (Robert Mitchum) to deal with a blackmailer.

Then came The Magic of Lassie, in which he played a vineyard owner attempting to reunite Lassie with his granddaughter. Its producer, Bonita Granville Wrather, who owned all of Lassie's rights, told me in 1977, "The film is going to bring Lassie back to a whole new generation." It's on TV all the time, but there hasn't been a film about Lassie in years. We have a great cast in this, including James Stewart, Mickey Rooney, Alice Faye, and Stephanie Zimbalist.' The film bombed when it was released in 1978. Star Wars and Superman were family favourites. Lassie was simply out of date. It was Jim's final Hollywood film, excluding television work.

'Things have changed in movies over the last few years,' he said in 1979, aged seventy-one. There are family movies, but they are all about special effects. Where are you going to send me in outer space? I'll keep looking for something to do, but I don't hold my breath. At my age, you don't want to hold your breath for longer than five seconds anyway . . . just in case the next breath doesn't come!'

The opportunity of something excellent finally looked like coming his way in 1979. Joshua Logan told Jim that he was bidding for the film rights to the Ernest Thompson play On Golden Pond, with the idea of casting Jim in it. Jim was delighted, but his delight turned to disappointment when Jane Fonda outbid all comers for the rights so she could star in it with her father. It was, in effect, a chance for daughter and father to finally get close. Jim understood, and he called Henry up to congratulate him. 'It was more important for Hank and Jane to make that film than it was for me,' he said. The film would be Fonda's crowning achievement, bringing him a Golden Globe and an Oscar in 1982.

Jim turned up in a bizarre Japanese production called The Green Horizon, released in 1981. Jim and Gloria had been visiting a Kenyan game reserve in 1979 where they came across the filmmakers, and Jim was persuaded to appear, speaking several lines. 'Never did understand what it was all about,' Jim told me. 'I was just some old fella who loved animals and living in the wild. I did it on a whim . . . thought it would help to promote wildlife conservation.'

In 1980 the best work Jim could find was a thirty-minute TV film called Mr. Krueger's Christmas. He played the janitor of an apartment block who is alone at Christmas time. But his Christmas becomes complete thanks to the intervention of a little girl. The film was actually produced by the Church of Jesus Christ of Latter-day Saints (the Mormons) and was an uplifting story about the true meaning of Christmas. Jim and Gloria stayed in Salt Lake City and socialised with the Mormon hierarchy, much to the displeasure of the Presbyterian Church. But as Jim said, 'It was just about faith in God and knowing what Christmas is really about–and that's the same in any Christian faith.'

What Jim probably never knew was that the Mormons stuck a five-minute epilogue on the end to invite people to join their church–although this version was purely for use by Mormon missionaries and was not seen when the film aired on American television.

In February 1980, the American Film Institute (AFI) honoured Stewart with its Life Achievement Award. The cream of Hollywood turned out for the occasion: Gene Kelly, Jack Lemmon, William Holden, Charlton Heston, Stefanie Powers, Walter Matthau, Richard Widmark, Karl Malden–and, of course, Henry Fonda in the role of Master of Ceremonies. Among the younger generation of actors was Dustin Hoffman.

A montage of scenes from Stewart's films opened the proceedings, including the box-office flop that became a legend, It's a Wonderful Life, the always-loved Harvey, the once derided but now revered The Spirit of St. Louis, and the previously revealed Anatomy of a Murder. Then Henry Fonda stepped to the podium. Two years earlier, Fonda had been the AFI's Life Achievement recipient. He waved to Stewart and said, 'Glad it's you, Jim . . . in the hot seat! Gloria, hold his hand and make him enjoy it.' Some of Stewart's co-stars had their say, including Widmark, Malden and Ruth Hussey, as did some of Hollywood's most legendary directors including Henry

Hathaway and Mervyn LeRoy.

Next, Dustin Hoffman took the stage. He talked of how his own father had worked at Columbia Studios when Mr. Smith Goes to Washington was being filmed. Telling Stewart, 'My father grew up with you,' he continued, 'I only saw It's a Wonderful Life two days ago. I'm the only one up here representing my generation of actors. When I saw you on screen in that performance, you made me laugh, you made me cry, and you made me wish for a country which perhaps we haven't seen for a while. Let me just say in closing that you made my parents very happy, you have made me very happy and I'm sure you're going to make my children very happy. And if this world has any Capra luck, you're going to make my children's children very happy.'

'Although Jim was happy to see all of his friends--all of his surviving friends--the tribute from Hoffman meant more to him than anything else said--well, nearly anything,' Gloria explained. Jim, on the other hand, would express his gratitude with his customary warm and honest smile, but he would never reveal the overpowering feeling he was battling to prevent from bursting to the surface.'

Finally, AFI chairman George Stevens Jr. called the guest of honour up to the stage to accept his prize. Stewart began by expressing his gratitude, 'Thank you everyone for sharing such a great evening... which is about to go bad as I... struggling around for the perfect words to communicate my thankfulness.' Stewart, on the other hand, was not fumbling at all. Every word he said pleased the audience. 'I realise it's late, and I told myself I'd talk quickly so I wouldn't keep you awake any longer than necessary. The trouble is... I don't know how to speak quickly!' Jimmy Stewart, a very fortunate fella, was how he described his life, career, and Life Achievement Award.

Jim's age was catching up with him by 1980. He was admitted to the hospital for five days due to an abnormal heartbeat. That same year, he was struck by sciatica, which prevented him from attending a picture exhibition in New York to benefit African conservation efforts.

Jim had to give up one of his biggest interests in 1981. 'I had to give up flying, which was a great letdown because I loved flying more than anything,' he stated. I used to own the Piper Club, and I enjoyed being there. I could fly out there in my tiny plane, fly up over the mountains, and land on the tiny strips ranchers had laid out for me. But my hearing had deteriorated to the point that I couldn't understand what the tower was saying to me. They grew tired of having to repeat themselves, and I grew tired of having to ask them to do so. So, after forty-five years, I had to give it up.'

'It just got too unsafe to have him flying about up there, isolated from the rest of the world,' Gloria explained. He'd never be able to drive a car, but he could always fly a plane. But when he couldn't hear what people were saying to him over the radio, he was a risk to himself, others, and my nerves.'

When Henry Fonda received his Best Actor Oscar for On Golden Pond, he was too sick to leave his Bel Air home, so his daughter Jane accepted it on his behalf. Jim visited Fonda on a regular basis; Hank lay in bed, Jim sat by him, and they remained in quiet for extended periods of time. 'I just couldn't believe I was losing my very best buddy,' Jim subsequently told me.

Gloria claimed that because both men were deaf, they had to shout at each other when they spoke. 'That made Hank laugh,' she commented. 'Yeah, it sure did,' Jim muttered quietly enough that I couldn't hear him.

Fonda died on August 11, 1982. Jim immediately rushed to Fonda's house to be with the family, which included Jane and Hank's widow

Shirlee. Gloria later learned that Jim sat silently in an armchair, lost in meditation, while others conversed. After a time, he exclaimed, 'It was the biggest kite we ever flew.' Then he told the Fondas about how he and Hank had flown kites, and after he finished, he was silent again.

In 1982, Jim was provided a chance to deliver a truly amazing performance--"much like Hank did in On Golden Pond," he remarked. Right of Way was a Home Box Office (HBO) TV film based on a play by Richard Lees (who also co-produced the film version) about an elderly couple who decide to commit suicide despite their daughter's wishes. Bette Davis was cast in the role of his wife. Gloria claimed Jim was made to feel humiliated because the director, George Schaefer, and co-producer, Philip Parslow, insisted on his taking a physical "to prove he wouldn't drop dead halfway through production."

The production began in October 1982. Jim was not only expecting to accomplish a professional high point, but he was also paying tribute to Henry Fonda in his own unique way. After completing scenes that physically and emotionally strained him, he would turn to the sky and exclaim, 'That's for you, Hank.'

But Right of Way was not going to be the adventure Jim had planned for. Although he would never acknowledge it publicly, he despised working with Bette Davis. 'She thought the movie was just about her,' Gloria explained. 'She never gave Jim a chance.' Jim had to kiss Davis on the cheek while filming a scene in which they were lying in bed. 'When Jim moved to kiss her, she turned her head away,' Gloria said. Everyone, including Jim, was taken aback. So he just hugged her in the next take. I could have slapped him! But Jim kept his temper under control. I know the director felt the same way about how she handled him. The chemistry between Hank Fonda and Katy Hepburn in On Golden Pond should have been there. However, there was no chemistry. She simply locked him out, and the film suffered as a result.'

Two different endings were filmed. In one, dubbed the "happy ending," the pair succeeds in their suicide attempt; in the other, dubbed the "unhappy ending," the police arrive in time to arrest them. Jim had always maintained that the 'happy ending' was the only one that was correct. 'We viewed the film for the first time in a private screening,' Gloria recounted. The first thing we observed was that the film had been trimmed around Bette Davis, and much of Jim's performance had been lost as a result. Then, when the film came to a conclusion, it wasn't the finale Jim had hoped for. He was distraught since this was his last opportunity to flourish as an actor, and it had been snatched away from him. I stood there with him, crying. He didn't remark, "Don't cry in front of everyone," for once.

HBO was also dissatisfied with the ending, and while the network disputed with the director, the film was shelved. After a year, Jim suggested that they include a scene of the daughter smelling gas and realising her parents had died. The battle lines had been formed for so long that neither side appreciated the concept, but the insert had to be done in order for the film to be aired. That was the final version to be shown in 1983. Regardless of the final modification, Gloria felt the picture was marred by Bette Davis' behaviour on set and "her bullying of the director into making it her film."

Throughout the 1980s, Jim received numerous prizes and honours, including those from the Cannes Film Festival, the United Service Organizations (USO), the Boy Scouts of America, Indiana University, and the Museum of the Moving Image in New York. He was invited to the Berlin Film Festival in 1982 to be honoured with Joan Fontaine. In May of the following year, he spent his 75th birthday in Indiana, where he and Gloria travelled in a motorcade along Philadelphia Street and attended the dedication of a statue of Jim outside the courthouse. The statue was facing the former hardware shop, which now housed the Savings & Trust Bank.

Jim was also honoured for his career achievements at the Kennedy Center in Washington in 1983. 'I don't seem to be making movies any longer,' Jim said to me a few years later. I just earn a lot of prizes and recognition for creating 'em.'

The abnormal pulse resurfaced the next year, and Jim was placed with a pacemaker. Only a few weeks later, he was back in the hospital for skin cancer radiation treatment. The treatment was effective.

Another award came in 1985, when the Academy of Motion Picture Arts and Sciences bestowed upon him an honorary Oscar. Cary Grant invited him up stage to receive his trophy. Frank Capra and other filmmakers were thanked for "so generously and brilliantly guiding me through the no-man's-land of my own intentions." That same year, he received a Medal of Freedom, and the decade's honours were capped by an award from the Lincoln Center in 1990.

Jim had one more television appearance in 1986, in the Civil War drama North and South, Book 2. It was only a cameo as a Southern lawyer. The scripts then stopped arriving entirely. Jim spent a significant amount of time reading books and publications. He quit golf and told his golfing buddies, 'Look, fellas, the reality is, I don't like golf.'

Gloria, one of Jim's friends, suggested that he try flying a glider. However, during his one and only flight, Jim discovered that he couldn't manage the glider like he could an airliner, and his companion had to take control immediately before they crashed. Gloria believed Jim panicked because he was frustrated by his inability to operate a real jet.

Jim had been jotting tiny poems for years, and in 1989 a collection of them was released by Crown Books under the title Jimmy Stewart and His Poems. Jim and Gloria went on a book tour to promote the book, which was released in time for Christmas 1989 in New York, Washington, Chicago, and Dallas. For the 81-year-old actor, the tour proved exhausting. Many people commented on how frail and skinny he appeared, but Gloria, now seventy, viewed it as her job to keep him going for as long as she could.

In 1991, Jim was ecstatic when he was approached to work on an animated feature film. He gave the voice of a lawman named Wylie Burp in An American Tail: Fievel Goes West. Except for revivals of classic films, it was the last time that legendary voices would be heard in a cinema.

Gloria's lung cancer diagnosis in 1993 was the biggest shock of Jim's life. I recall her telling me the news over the phone; as usual, she refused to make the situation sound overly dramatic: 'You know me, Michael. I'd die if I didn't smoke two packs of cigarettes a day.' She told me that Jim had been pressing her to have chemotherapy, and I urged that she do it as well.

She finally received chemo, and almost immediately her hair began to come out and she became severely ill. She informed me that when she asked her physicians if the chemo would genuinely save her life, they ultimately conceded that it would simply extend it. 'I'm not going to lose all my hair and be sick all the time just to survive a few more months,' she said, so I told them no more chemotherapy. I want to make the most of the time I have left. Jim understands and agrees with me.'

Gloria died on February 16, 1994. She was seventy-five. She had always seemed so much younger to me. Over the years, whenever I called the Stewart residence, Gloria had always answered. When I attempted calling to convey my sympathies, nobody responded. So I sent a message and arranged for flowers to be delivered.

Jim was never heard from or spoke to again. He retired and became a recluse. Except for his family, few people saw him. I eventually learned that Jim was no longer seeing any of his old buddies. Gloria had been the focal point of his life, and now she was gone. 'If the moment comes when my life has no more purpose, I won't cling on to it,' Jim once said. I'm not going to fight God if he wants to take me.'

Indiana honoured Jim once more on May 20, 1995, with the launch of the Jimmy Stewart Museum. This took up the entire top level of the Philadelphia Street municipal library. Jim declined to attend the festivities, preferring to live in seclusion; instead, his twin daughters represented him. He was, in effect, honoured in some way virtually to the end. 'Awards and honours are beautiful things... but I sure wish they'd given them to me when I was younger,' he once commented to me. It's difficult for an old guy like me to go from one ceremony to the next.'

Jim feel at home during the 1995 Christmas vacation and hit his head. The press stories made it appear worse than it was, and he was discharged home after a few days in the hospital for observation. All of this presents a quite pitiful picture of such a beloved man. I believe he was a happy recluse rather than a sad one. He'd always been able to be alone. If he stayed at home all the time, it was partly due to Gloria's absence, which forced him to get up and go out. It was also the man's age, which was approaching ninety.

He had known for some time that his God would eventually call him, and on July 2, 1997, He did. Jim passed away peacefully in his sleep. Hollywood mourned, as did his family and much of the rest of the globe. A small military guard of honour was present for the funeral at the local Presbyterian Church. His ashes were later interred in Forest Lawn Memorial Park in Glendale, California.

It was heartbreaking to lose such a beloved and esteemed man. He will be much missed not only by those who knew him personally, but also by everyone who enjoys watching movies. And yet, like all great cinema stars, he left a legacy of films for future generations to appreciate, some fantastic, some good, some not so good, but all imbued with the peculiar enchantment that made James Stewart a star.

But, for Jim, it was the 'small chunks of time' that he felt would be his lasting legacy when he died, not the films. When I asked him once how he wanted to be remembered, he didn't take long to come up with an answer--as if he'd known it for years. 'I hope people will say things like, "I remember this film where Jimmy Stewart was dancing with some girl, and the floor opened up and underneath was a swimming pool, and they fell in," he remarked. (This is a scene from the film It's a Wonderful Life.) 'It doesn't matter if they can't remember the name of the film; what matters is that it made them happy for a couple of minutes, and they always recalled it,' he concluded. It's a beautiful thing to be able to offer them little bits of time to remember. "Yeah, Jimmy Stewart, he gave us little pieces of time," I want people to say.

Jimmy Stewart provided us all a lot of small chunks of time.

Printed in Great Britain
by Amazon